THOMAS R. SCHREINER

# RUN
## TO WIN
# THE PRIZE

PERSEVERANCE IN THE NEW TESTAMENT

APOLLOS (an imprint of Inter-Varsity Press)
Norton Street, Nottingham NG7 3HR, England
*Email: ivp@ivpbooks.com*
*Website: www.ivpbooks.com*

© Thomas R. Schreiner

*First published 2009*

**British Library Cataloguing in Publication Data**
A catalogue record for this book is available from the British Library.

UK ISBN: 978-1-84474-369-8

Set in Monotype Garamond 11/14pt
Typeset in Great Britain by Servis Filmsetting Ltd, Stockport, Cheshire
Printed and bound in Great Britain by Ashford Colour Press Ltd, Gosport,
Hampshire

Inter-Varsity Press publishes Christian books that are true to the Bible and
that communicate the gospel, develop discipleship and strengthen the church
for its mission in the world.

Inter-Varsity Press is closely linked with the Universities and Colleges
Christian Fellowship, a student movement connecting Christian Unions in
universities and colleges throughout Great Britain, and a member movement
of the International Fellowship of Evangelical Students.
Website: *www.uccf.org.uk*

# CONTENTS

# FOREWORD

One of the most spectacular walks in the Lake District is Striding Edge. It is a long, narrow crest of mountain, with the ground dropping sharply away on either side. It is wonderful to walk along, but there is always the thought that one cannot stray too far either side. In some ways, the doctrine of perseverance is rather like that. When understood and lived by correctly, it is breathtaking, but there are errors on either side.

On the one hand a Christian can downplay the significance of perseverance and biblical passages that warn of apostasy. The result can be a complacent faith, which responds only too feebly to assaults and temptations, if it responds at all.

On the other hand, a Christian can insist on the doctrine of perseverance in a way that makes it differ very little from a work which we contribute to our salvation. It can seem that God himself cannot save without the effort we bring. For some, that can breed habits of spiritual pride; for others, that can lead to doubt and insecurity, or even despair, since they are only too aware how far and how frequently they fall short of the standards of holiness God has set out.

Furthermore, some exegetically demanding passages of Scripture are at stake in these debates, and it is perhaps no great surprise that ministers are wary of teaching congregations about this subject. Yet, of course, it is very difficult for pastors of God's people not in effect to adopt some position on the perseverance.

It is therefore of great benefit to have Thomas Schreiner's reflections in this book, based on the lectures he delivered at the 2008 Oak Hill Theological College School of Theology. This is not the first time Professor Schreiner has addressed this subject (with Ardel B. Caneday he has written *The Race Set Before Us: A Biblical Theology of Perseverance and Assurance* [IVP, 2001]), but the present work provides the opportunity both for summary and for a tight focus on issues particularly prone to misunderstanding.

Professor Schreiner reminds us of some simple but profound biblical truths. To begin with, there is a difference between perfection and perseverance. Perfection is not possible before our glorification in Christ, and our present condition is marked by the way we are both justified and sinners, and must battle to put to death the deeds of the flesh.

Perseverance is Christ-focused, a sustained looking to him and to no other person and no other thing. It is intimately related to the faith through which we are saved. If faith is the open, empty hand that receives Christ, perseverance is keeping the hand open to Christ. Perseverance is not a work that we bring to finalize our salvation.

What role, then, do passages such as Hebrews 6 play in the life of the believer? Professor Schreiner points out that just as God is pleased sovereignly to call men and women to faith in Christ through human means, so too he preserves us through human means. The passages in question therefore are looking forward and are warnings, not descriptions of what has already taken place. Their purpose is to preserve and they are means by which God does so. Our prayer is that this book is likewise used as a human means by God to glorify himself by encouraging, warning and sustaining his people.

Mike Ovey
Oak Hill College

# PREFACE

I want to examine in this book what I explored with Ardel Caneday in a more thorough way in a book titled *The Race Set Before Us*.[1] Why is another book necessary if a previous book has already been published? First, the length and comprehensiveness of the previous book have been off-putting to some, and as a result the thesis of the book has not been accessible to all. My hope is that the current book will bring some of the central themes of the previous work to a wider audience. Where this book seems too brief, I would point the reader to the longer work. Second, some have misunderstood what we were arguing for in *The Race Set Before Us*. Despite what we specifically set forth in the book, some have thought that we were proposing works-righteousness, an unreachable perfectionism, or even that true believers could fall from salvation by committing apostasy.[2] Such conclusions directly contradict the previous work, and thus I think it will be helpful to consider the issues again in a less technical format, in order to

---

1. See Thomas R. Schreiner and Ardel B. Caneday, *The Race Set Before Us: A Biblical Theology of Perseverance and Assurance* (Downers Grove: InterVarsity Press; Leicester: Inter-Varsity Press, 2001).
2. I am thinking here of a number of conversations I have had with readers of the book, not necessarily of published responses.

provide further clarification of some controversial issues. In other
words, another book is warranted because it will provide a fresh
and somewhat different angle to the questions explored in *The Race
Set Before Us*. In particular, I hope from time to time in this work
to consider more directly the pastoral implications of the warnings and admonitions found in the NT.[3] The role of admonitions
and warnings is immensely practical in living out the Christian
life, for it relates to the assurance of believers. Further, the study
has important consequences for ministry, since it addresses how
we should counsel believers from the Scriptures.

Nick Nowalk deserves special thanks for some quotations
he sent me from stalwarts in church history. These quotations
have proved to be invaluable for the argument of the book.
I am also grateful to Greg Van Court for his careful proofing
of the manuscript and for producing the Scripture index. Greg's
work and joyful spirit have refreshed my spirit. I am grateful to
Oak Hill Theological College for inviting me to give the lectures
upon which this book is based. I enjoyed my time at Oak Hill
immensely, and profited from my conversations and discussions
with both students and faculty. I am particularly grateful to Chris
Green for graciously hosting my wife and me during our stay.

3. The OT is omitted for space reasons, but we find the same urgent warnings in the OT. The constant presence of warnings and admonitions in
the NT means that we cannot examine all the texts even in the NT.

# ABBREVIATIONS

| | |
|---|---|
| AB | Anchor Bible |
| *BBR* | *Bulletin for Biblical Research* |
| BECNT | Baker's Exegetical Commentary on the New Testament |
| BNTC | Black's New Testament Commentaries |
| ConBNT | Coniectanea biblica, New Testament |
| ESV | English Standard Version |
| IBC | Interpretation Bible Commentary |
| ICC | International Critical Commentary |
| *JETS* | *Journal of the Evangelical Theological Society* |
| *JOTT* | *Journal of Translation and Textlinguistics* |
| JSNTSup. | *Journal for the Study of the New Testament* Supplement |
| LCC | Library of Christian Classics |
| NAC | New American Commentary |
| NASB | New American Standard Bible |
| NICNT | New International Commentary on the New Testament |
| NIGTC | New International Greek Testament Commentary |
| NT | New Testament |
| *NTS* | *New Testament Studies* |
| OT | Old Testament |

| | |
|---|---|
| SBT | Studies in Biblical Theology |
| SJT Occasional Paper | *Scottish Journal of Theology* Occasional Paper |
| SBLDS | Society for Biblical Literature, Dissertation Series |
| TNTC | Tyndale New Testament Commentary |
| *TrinJ* | *Trinity Journal* |
| WBC | Word Biblical Commentary |
| WEC | Wycliffe Exegetical Commentary |
| *WTJ* | *Westminster Theological Journal* |
| WUNT | Wissenschaftliche Untersuchungen zum Neuen Testament |

# 1. EXHORTATIONS TO PERSEVERE

Let me begin with two stories to illustrate the concerns of this book. Years ago, a young woman and her husband came to a Bible study I was leading. Two days after the Bible study they visited our house for dinner, and she expressed a keen desire to become a Christian. I was hesitant because she knew so little about the Christian faith. Nevertheless, I concluded that I might be resisting the Holy Spirit, and one thing led to another and she confessed Jesus as her Saviour that night in our living room. I assured her after her confession of faith that she was securely saved for ever: that nothing she did could remove her from the eternal life that was hers. Her husband shortly thereafter followed her in the same faith. They both grew rapidly in the faith during the next year, and we were regularly involved in Bible studies with them. But a year after her confession of faith, she changed dramatically. She decided to divorce her husband, quit attending church, and ceased going to Bible studies. I pleaded with her to at least go into counselling, but to no avail. All of this happened many years ago, and I have since lost all contact with her, though I know there was no change of mind or repentance in the next fifteen years.

The other story also relates to a friend who prayed with me to become a believer. I saw the radiance and joy in her life. She began to grow in remarkable ways. And yet, in a year or two the early bloom of her faith began to fade. She began to get drunk on a fairly regular basis. She ended up living with a person who was an adherent of Buddhism. On one occasion I said to her, 'By this we know that we have come to know him, if we keep his commandments' (1 John 2:3).[1] A number of years passed. She broke off the relationship with the first man and ended up getting married to another. Still no desire for the things of God and Jesus Christ manifested itself. And yet, after a few years of marriage, a change began to take place. Her desire to follow the Lord resurfaced, and she began to read Scripture, pray and take seriously her church involvement. Once again she began to talk to me about spiritual matters. She gave every indication that she belonged to Jesus Christ and that she loved him. A significant period of time had intervened between her first confession of faith and the return to her first love. Was her first experience a sham, so that she was truly saved the second time? Or did she lose her salvation and regain it later? Or was she a believer the entire time, with a temporary lapse in her faith and obedience?

In this book I intend to offer some advice as to what we should say in the situations I have sketched in above. But I am not only speaking to these particular situations, for the argument of this book is that all believers everywhere need the warnings and admonitions of Scripture.

--------

1. All Scripture quotations are from the ESV, unless specified otherwise.

## What do we say to new Christians?

In the first story I related above, I told the new believer that she was saved no matter what she did. Is this a proper way to speak to new believers? When we look at the NT, what did the apostles and early Christian teachers say to new believers? Surely their words function as paradigms and models for us. When Barnabas arrived in Syrian Antioch, after hearing that many Gentiles in Antioch had embraced the gospel and turned to the Lord, he responded with joy. 'When he [Barnabas] came and saw the grace of God, he was glad, and he exhorted them all to remain faithful to the Lord with steadfast purpose' (Acts 11:23). Barnabas recognized that the conversion of the Gentiles in Antioch was a work of God's grace and could not be finally attributed to human agency. Still, a focus on God's grace does not preclude the need for warnings and admonitions, but is the foundation for calling upon believers to persevere. Barnabas summoned his hearers to remain and persevere (*prosmenein*) in their relationship with the Lord. Indeed, they are to do so 'with steadfast purpose', so that the focus is on the commitment required of these new believers.

A similar scenario played out when Paul and Barnabas evangelized in Pisidian Antioch. Once again a number of people responded positively to the proclamation of the gospel. What advice did Paul and Barnabas give to these new converts? 'And after the meeting of the synagogue broke up, many Jews and devout converts to Judaism followed Paul and Barnabas, who, as they spoke with them, urged them to continue in the grace of God' (Acts 13:43). Two parallels to Acts 11:23 stand out. First, the new believers are 'urged' to persevere. In Acts 11:23 the verb 'exhort' (*parakalein*) is used, whereas here we find the word 'persuade' (*peithein*), translated 'urge' by the ESV. In both instances, the seriousness of the admonition is underscored by the verb, showing that vigilance is mandated for new believers. Second, the same verb used in Acts 11:23 is repeated. Believers are 'to continue (*prosmenein*) in the grace of God'. The ongoing commitment of believers to their new-found faith is emphasized. Third, both texts refer to God's grace. Believers are not exhorted to trust in themselves or to continue in the faith by virtue of their own efforts. They are to continue the Christian life in the same manner they began it: by the faith given to them by God's grace. Hence, the perseverance called for here should not be understood as works-righteousness. Instead, it is nothing other than a continual reliance upon the grace of God. We are reminded of what Paul taught in Gal. 3:3. We continue in the Christian life in the same way we began, for we do not initiate the Christian life in the Spirit and progress in it by means of the flesh.

At the conclusion of the first missionary journey of Paul and Barnabas (Acts 13–14), they revisited the cities in which they had planted churches. The instruction given to such new converts, which Luke records in a compact manner (Acts 14:22–23), is surely significant. Besides appointing elders and praying for them, we are told that they strengthened the new disciples by 'encouraging them to continue in the faith, and saying that through many tribulations we must enter the kingdom of God' (Acts 14:22). We receive insight here into why these new believers were exhorted 'to continue' (*emmenein*) in their recently confessed faith, for entrance into the kingdom will be preceded by many difficulties and sufferings. Such 'tribulations' may deflect believers from continuing in the faith they embraced, enticing them to a life that promises comfort and relief. A pattern is evident in the exhortations given to new believers, especially when we recognize the brevity of what Luke includes in his account. Recent Christians are not told that they will inherit the kingdom no matter what they do. Rather, they are urged to remain and continue in the faith.

Another window into what the apostles and early Christian leaders taught new believers is provided by 1 Thess. 3:1–5. What Paul teaches here accords with what Luke includes in the text we just examined (Acts 14:22–23), for the tribulations encountered by the Thessalonians raised concerns about whether they continued to believe. Paul sent Timothy to the newly established

Thessalonian church, for he knew they were disturbed by the trials and difficulties that they had experienced since their conversion. In verse 5 Paul explains why he sent Timothy: 'For this reason, when I could bear it no longer, I sent to learn about your faith, for fear that somehow the tempter had tempted you and our labour would be in vain.' Paul was worried that the Thessalonians had abandoned their faith in Christ because of the intensity of persecution. Satan, he feared, had subverted their faith, and hence his 'labour' in planting the church would have been wasted if the Thessalonians had forsaken their faith. Paul did not assume that the Thessalonians were truly believers merely because they had embraced the faith when he first preached to them. The authenticity of their faith manifested itself in their response to trials, so that their persistence in faith demonstrated whether their faith was genuine.

Other texts could be included at this point, but no attempt is made here to be comprehensive. What I hope is clear is that new believers were regularly instructed after their conversion about the need to persevere in the faith.

## What do we say to experienced Christians?

We have seen above that recent converts are exhorted to continue in the faith, but such an exhortation is not limited to new believers. The exhortation to persevere until the end is a staple of NT teaching. It is part of the warp and woof of NT parenesis. For example, Peter sums up his entire letter in 1 Pet. 5:12,[2] remarking that he has exhorted and declared to them 'the true grace of God'. Then follows the admonition addressed to churches facing

---

2. E. R. Wendland argues that the aim of the entire letter is summed up here. '"Stand Fast in the True Grace of God!" A Study of 1 Peter', *JOTT* 13 (2000), pp. 25–26.

persecution: 'Stand firm in it.' In other words, they are to stand
fast in God's grace in the midst of their troubles. The devil is on
the prowl, attempting 'to devour' and destroy believers (1 Pet. 5:8).
And the devil aims to shatter the faith of believers by inducing
them to commit apostasy.[3] Believers will not commit apostasy
and fall away if they 'resist' the devil by being 'firm in [their] faith'
(1 Pet. 5:9). Peter does not exhort the readers to do something
unusual or surprising at the onset of persecution. Rather, they are
to continue trusting in God for strength to face the pressures and
persecution that afflict them. Some of the same themes considered
earlier appear again here. Believers in the Petrine churches may be
tempted to disown Christ because of the intensity of persecution.
Hence, Peter admonishes them to remain vigilant and faithful.

Similarly, Jude commands believers to 'keep [themselves] in the
love of God' (Jude 21), responding to a situation in which false
teachers had slipped into the church under cover and were promot-
ing destructive teachings and licentious behaviour. In the context
of Jude, keeping themselves in God's love functions as the converse
of apostasy. Either believers remain in God's love, or they fall away
from the faith and follow the lifestyle and teachings of the inter-
lopers. No other option exists. Jude does not merely give helpful
advice on growth in the Christian life. Keeping oneself in the love
of God is essential for receiving eternal life on the final day.[4]

---

3. Rightly, Leonard Goppelt, *A Commentary on I Peter*, ed. by F. Hahn; trans.
   and augmented by J. E. Alsup (Grand Rapids: Eerdmans, 1993), p. 361;
   J. N. D. Kelly, *A Commentary on the Epistles of Peter and Jude* (Thornapple
   Commentaries, reprint; Grand Rapids: Baker, 1981), p. 210.

4. See here the remarks of Jonathan Edwards about perseverance: "'Tis
   necessary to salvation as a necessary consequence and evidence of a
   title to salvation. There never is a title to salvation without it. Though it
   han't the righteousness by which a title to life is attained, yet none have
   that righteousness that don't persevere; and that because although it is
   not proper to say that perseverance is necessary in order to justification,

The need to persevere also appears in Hebrews, and indeed the call to continue in the faith informs the entire letter. Hence many texts could be selected from the letter in support of what is argued for here. Here I cite only one verse: 'See to it that no one fails to obtain the grace of God' (Heb. 12:15). Such failure cannot be restricted merely to a lack of vitality or fruitfulness in the Christian life, for the author immediately considers the case of Esau (Heb. 12:16–17) as an example of someone who repudiated the blessings he enjoyed.[5] To fall short of God's grace, then, is another way of describing apostasy – irrevocable separation from God. A very similar command is directed to the Corinthians in Paul's second letter. They are 'not to receive the grace of God in vain' (2 Cor. 6:1). We can be quite sure that final salvation is in view here. First, the word 'vain' (*kenos*) in Paul is regularly associated with final judgment and destruction (cf. 1 Cor. 15:10, 14, 58; Gal. 2:2; Eph. 5:6; Phil. 2:16; Col. 2:8; 1 Thess. 2:1; 3:5). Second, in

---

yet a persevering principle is necessary in order to justification . . . 'Tis necessary that a man should believe in Christ, and cleave to Christ in a persevering way: a temporary faith don't justify. But in order to that, persons must have that faith that is of a persevering, everlasting sort. He must have that sort of seed that is an abiding seed. 'Tis not a vanishing but a durable faith that justifies.' 'Persevering Faith', in *The Works of Jonathan Edwards*, vol. 19, ed. by M. X. Lesser (New Haven: Yale University Press, 2001), pp. 600–601. I would nuance what Edwards says a bit differently, but he rightly sees that persevering faith is required for final salvation.

5. Rightly, Grant R. Osborne, 'A Classical Arminian View', in Herbert W. Bateman IV (ed.), *Four Views on the Warning Passages in Hebrews* (Grand Rapids: Kregel, 2007), p. 123; Gareth Lee Cockerill, 'A Wesleyan Arminian View', in Herbert W. Bateman IV (ed.), *Four Views on the Warning Passages in Hebrews* (Grand Rapids: Kregel, 2007), pp. 285–286. Against, Randall C. Gleason, 'A Moderate Reformed View', in Herbert W. Bateman IV (ed.), *Four Views on the Warning Passages in Hebrews* (Grand Rapids: Kregel, 2007), p. 169.

context the Corinthians are exhorted to 'be reconciled to God' (2 Cor. 5:20), which is defined in terms of the forgiveness of sins (2 Cor. 5:19). Indeed, in 2 Cor. 6:2 Paul immediately follows up the need 'not to receive the grace of God in vain' with the claim that 'now is the day of salvation'. Hence there are good reasons to think that the exhortation relates to final salvation. In both Heb. 12:15 and 2 Cor. 6:1, readers are implored to continue to respond to God's grace in order to obtain the final reward on the last day.[6]

I conclude this initial foray by considering Phil. 2:16. Believers must '[hold] fast the word of life, so that in the day of Christ I may be proud that I did not run in vain or labour in vain'. Believers are exhorted to hold fast the gospel they initially embraced until the day of Christ. The general nature of the command suggests that the admonition to persevere applies to all believers, so that the exhortation here cannot be limited to the Philippian situation. Some scholars maintain, however, that the participle 'holding fast' (*epechontes*) should be translated 'holding forth' instead of 'holding fast'. In other words, the verse relates to evangelism instead of perseverance.[7] Vern Poythress

---

6. Calvin himself also believed perseverance was necessary for final salvation. 'Still, our redemption would be imperfect if he did not lead us ever onward to the final goal of salvation. Accordingly, the moment we turn away even slightly from him, our salvation, which rests firmly in him, gradually vanishes away. As a result, all those who do not repose in him voluntarily deprive themselves of all grace.' John Calvin, *Institutes of the Christian Religion*, ed. by John T. McNeill, trans. and indexed by Ford Lewis Battles (LCC; Philadelphia: Westminster, 1960), 2.16.1. Even though Calvin here rightly emphasizes the need to persevere, he does not express the idea well, and his words could be understood to demand a kind of perfection which would undermine assurance.

7. Robert L. Plummer, *Paul's Understanding of the Church's Mission: Did the Apostle Paul Expect the Early Christian Communities to Evangelize?* (Paternoster Biblical Monographs; Waynesboro, GA: Paternoster, 2006), pp. 74–77.

has argued that we cannot exclude either meaning, with the result that the term includes both the idea of evangelism and perseverance.[8] Poythress may be correct in arguing that both meanings are in view. I want to defend here the idea that perseverance is also in view. First, twice Paul speaks of working 'in vain' in the verse. As noted previously, the idea of a vain or futile ministry occurs when Paul considers the possibility of believers not continuing in the faith.[9] Second, the warning against grumbling and complaining (Phil. 2:14) harks back to the OT and the grumbling of the wilderness generation (Exod. 16:7, 8, 9, 12; Num. 17:5, 10) and their failure to enter the promised land.[10] The land promise in Exodus becomes a type of the future inheritance in Paul,[11] and hence a connection is forged between Israel's failure to enter the land of promise and the warning directed to believers.[12] Third, the words 'blameless', 'innocent' and 'without

---

8. Vern Sheridan Poythress, '"Hold Fast" Versus "Hold Out" in Philippians 2:16', *WTJ* 63 (2002), pp. 45–53.

9. See also 1 Cor. 15:2; Gal. 3:4; 4:11, where the same notion is expressed with the word 'vain' (*eikē*).

10. Phil. 2:14 is the first verse of a long sentence that concludes with v. 16. Hence it is vital in considering the meaning of v. 16.

11. A difficult question is whether Israel in the wilderness or Esau are considered to be damned. There may be a one-to-one correspondence between the OT and the NT, so that the wilderness generation and Esau are damned, and the same threat is held out against those who commit apostasy in the NT. On the other hand, it is also possible that the earthly punishments inflicted upon the wilderness generation and Esau now correspond to eternal punishment in the NT. In this latter view, there is an escalation between the type and the fulfilment. For the purposes of our discussion here, there is no need to resolve this matter. What is imperative is to see that those who fall away in the NT are threatened with eternal damnation.

12. For a study on inheritance in the OT, Jewish tradition and the NT, see James D. Hester, *Paul's Concept of Inheritance: A Contribution to the*

blemish' are in the same semantic range and are used elsewhere
in Paul to denote the godly character needed to obtain the final
reward.[13] Fourth, the expression 'that you may be . . . children
of God' (Phil. 2:15) has an eschatological reference, designating
the truth that those who continue to believe will be God's children on the day of Christ. Such an interpretation is confirmed
by the allusion to Deut. 32:5, which again considers the rebellion
of Israel. 'They [Israel] have dealt corruptly with him; / they
are no longer his children because they are blemished; / they
are a crooked and twisted generation.' Notice that Israel's sin
demonstrates they are not God's children, but Paul admonishes
the Philippians to hold fast the word of life so that they will be
God's children. Moreover, Israel was blemished, but the church
should remain unblemished. Finally, Israel was 'a crooked and
twisted generation', but the Philippians are to distinguish themselves as righteous in the midst of such an evil generation. The
many points of contact between Deut. 32:5 and Phil. 2:15 indicate that we have a call to perseverance in these verses. Finally,
the call to 'shine as lights in the world' probably alludes to Dan.
12:3, where believers are to shine like lights. Those believers who
shine like lights will 'be delivered' (Dan. 12:1). They will rise 'to
everlasting life' (Dan. 12:2). Hence we have another piece of evidence supporting the claim that Paul exhorts the Philippians to
continue in the faith to the end in order to receive the end-time
reward of eternal life.

---

Footnote 12 (*cont.*)

> *Understanding of Heilsgeschichte* (SJT Occasional Papers 14; Edinburgh:
> Oliver & Boyd, 1968). Hester remarks that Paul does not restrict the
> promise to the land of Canaan but widens it to include the entire world,
> and such a universal inheritance is tied to the work of Christ (pp.
> 77–78).

13. For 'blameless', see 1 Thess. 3:13. For 'without blemish', see Eph. 1:4;
    5:27; Col. 1:22.

## Conclusion

I have argued briefly here that we have indications in exhortations given to both new believers and experienced believers that perseverance is required to obtain eternal life.[14] NT authors did not promise an eschatological reward regardless of how someone lived in the future. Instead, we have seen that both new believers and experienced believers are urged to persevere to receive eternal life. The varied examples given here suggest that this was a commonplace in NT teaching. In the next chapter we are going to consider the many exhortations given to believers in the NT in which they are warned that if they fall away they will face eternal judgment.

---

14. Such a statement does not deny that believers already enjoy eternal life. We have an example here of the 'already but not yet' tension that pervades the NT. Believers already have eternal life, but will experience it in its fullness when Christ returns.

## 2. HOW TO UNDERSTAND THE WARNINGS IN SCRIPTURE

### The Landscape

I shall attempt to show in this chapter that warnings threatening final judgment are pervasive in Scripture. Severe warnings cannot be restricted to Hebrews, though the warning passages in Hebrews are particularly bracing and emphatic. Before analysing the biblical text, we should survey the scholarly landscape relative to the warning passages. First, many scholars maintain that the warnings in Scripture threaten believers with damnation if they fall away from the faith or apostatize. On this view the warnings are addressed to believers who have truly embraced Jesus Christ. They threaten final damnation if one apostatizes, and it is argued that true believers may indeed fall away from the faith.[1]

---

1. See I. H. Marshall, *Kept by the Power of God: A Study of Perseverance and*

If apostasy were not possible, they maintain, then why would the warnings be included? Warnings are superfluous if it is impossible to fall away. In the history of interpretation this view is identified as the Arminian interpretation.

A second view that has gained some popularity in recent years is the loss of rewards view. This view has been promoted in the United States by the Grace Evangelical Society and its journal, *Grace Evangelical Journal*.[2] According to this interpretation, the warnings are addressed to genuine believers. Failure to heed the warnings, however, will not lead to final judgment. Instead, believers will lose rewards if they fail to do what is commanded. The rewards in view are not eternal life, for eternal life is guaranteed and can never be lost by a believer. The rewards are blessings and privileges above and beyond eternal life, so that one who heeds the warnings will perhaps enjoy a higher status in heaven, or greater responsibility in heaven, because of their obedience. Often those who subscribe to this interpretation emphasize that if believers heed the warnings then they will also enjoy a more fruitful life as Christians on earth. They will be disciples who bear fruit and abide in Christ, enjoying

---

*Falling Away* (1969; reprint, Minneapolis: Bethany Fellowship, 1974); Scot McKnight, 'The Warning Passages of Hebrews: A Formal Analysis and Theological Conclusions', *TrinJ* 13 (1992), pp. 21–59; John Wesley, *Explanatory Notes Upon the New Testament* (London: The Epworth Press, 1952), p. 551; Osborne, 'A Classical Arminian View', pp. 86–128; Cockerill, 'A Wesleyan Arminian View', pp. 257–292.

2. Charles Stanley, *Eternal Security: Can You Be Sure?* (Nashville: Thomas Nelson, 1990); R. T. Kendall, *Once Saved, Always Saved* (Chicago: Moody Press, 1983); Zane C. Hodges, *The Gospel Under Siege: A Study on Faith and Works* (Dallas: Redención Viva, 1981); idem, *Absolutely Free: A Biblical Reply to Lordship Salvation* (Dallas: Redención Viva, 1989 and Grand Rapids: Zondervan, 1989); Michael Eaton, *No Condemnation: A New Theology of Assurance* (Downers Grove: InterVarsity, 1995); Gleason, 'A Moderate Reformed View', pp. 336–377.

true fellowship with him. Failure to be a disciple or to bear fruit can never rob a believer of salvation, for salvation is irrevocable and can never be lost. Still, the warnings are genuine warnings, for believers may not obtain the rewards God promised, and their lives on earth may not bring much glory to God.

Both the Arminian and the loss of rewards views agree that the warnings are addressed to genuine believers. Further, the threats are not merely hypothetical. If believers flout the warnings, they will face the consequences of such disobedience. Still, the two views differ on the nature of the punishment. Arminians claim that the warnings threaten loss of salvation, whereas the view associated with the Grace Evangelical Society sees only a loss of rewards.

Many of those from a Calvinist persuasion have still another take on the warning texts. In many instances they read the warning passages, especially in Hebrews 6, as if they are addressed to those who are not Christians.[3] Those challenged are 'almost' Christians but are not authentically saved. Calvinists who read the warnings this way agree with Arminians that the threat is final judgment, not merely loss of rewards. Further, they concur that

3. See John Owen, *Hebrews: The Epistle of Warning* (Grand Rapids: Kregel, 1953), pp. 96–98. This work is an abridgement by M. J. Tyron of John Owen's *Exposition of the Epistle to the Hebrews*, originally published in eight volumes. Roger Nicole, 'Some Comments on Hebrews 6:4–6 and the Doctrine of the Perseverance of God with the Saints', in Gerald F. Hawthorne (ed.), *Current Issues in Biblical and Patristic Interpretation: Studies in Honor of Merrill C. Tenney Presented by his Former Students* (Grand Rapids: Eerdmans, 1975), pp. 355–364; Wayne Grudem, 'Perseverance of the Saints: A Case Study from the Warning Passages in Hebrews', in Thomas R. Schreiner and Bruce A. Ware (eds), *Still Sovereign* (Grand Rapids: Baker, 2000), pp. 133–182; Buist M. Fanning, 'A Classical Reformed View', in Herbert W. Bateman IV (ed.), *Four Views on the Warning Passages in Hebrews* (Grand Rapids: Kregel, 2007), pp. 172–219.

the warnings are not hypothetical. Some actually do fall away and renounce the faith. Still, these warnings (at least in Hebrews 6) are addressed to those who are not genuine Christians, so there is no question of true believers forsaking their salvation.

## Introduction to Warnings

The intent of this chapter is not to analyse carefully the various views sketched in above. Instead, the biblical text will be consulted in order to demonstrate that warnings to believers pervade the NT. In other words, warning passages are not limited to Hebrews but are found in every corpus in the NT. Hence the interpretation of such texts is not confined to the controversial texts in Hebrews but confronts us often in the NT writings. Given the brevity of this book, selected warning texts will be examined in the Gospels, Paul, 2 Peter, 2 John, Revelation and Hebrews. I hope that enough texts are included here to show that warnings are fundamental to the gospel preached by early Christians. Along the way, I will also interact with the loss of reward view and the 'almost Christian' view sketched in above. Such interaction, however, will be limited and representative. In other words, I will not interact with these two views in every text, but will try to explain sufficiently why such interpretations are unconvincing. The problems with the loss of salvation view will be addressed at a later point, and not in our discussion of these texts.

## Warnings in the Gospels

Two warnings from the Gospels will be examined. Jesus, in addressing his disciples regarding their mission, declares: 'So everyone who acknowledges me before men, I also will acknowledge before my Father who is in heaven, but whoever denies me before men, I also will deny before my Father who is in heaven'

(Matt. 10:32–33). Clearly, Jesus speaks to all his disciples here, so the text cannot be confined to those who are almost Christians. The decision facing the disciples is starkly put. Either they acknowledge Jesus before others or they deny him. If they confess him as Lord and Christ, he will acknowledge them as belonging to him before the Father. If, on the other hand, they repudiate and deny him, then he will disavow them before the Father. It seems quite clear in the context that the penalty threatened is not merely loss of rewards but final judgment: being excluded from the Father's gracious presence. Such a view is confirmed by the remainder of the discourse, for Jesus also affirms that only 'the one who endures to the end will be saved' (Matt. 10:22).[4] Conversely, then, those who fail to continue in the faith will be destroyed. Further, Jesus claims that those who prize family members above him are 'not worthy' of him (Matt. 10:37).[5] And only those who take up the cross and follow him are 'worthy' of him (Matt. 10:38). In other words, only those who follow Jesus in discipleship will receive an eternal reward. It is difficult to believe that those who are unworthy of Jesus and refuse to follow him as disciples will receive an eternal reward. In one sense, of course, no one is worthy before God. Only those who receive the grace of God are saved, but we must beware of imposing such a teaching onto this context here. Indeed, verse 39 demonstrates that eternal life is at stake: 'Whoever finds his life will lose it, and whoever loses his life for my sake will find it' (Matt. 10:39). Only those who repudiate their lives for the sake of Jesus will gain them on the final day. Jesus, then, warns us as disciples in Matt. 10:32–33 not to deny him before men, for if we do so, then we will be damned at the final judgment.

---

4. The participle is conditional here. See Daniel B. Wallace, *Greek Grammar Beyond the Basics: An Exegetical Syntax of the New Testament* (Grand Rapids: Zondervan, 1996), p. 688.

5. Cf. Donald A. Hagner, *Matthew 1–13* (WBC; Dallas: Word, 1993), 292.

The second example from the Gospels comes from John 15:6: 'If anyone does not abide in me he is thrown away like a branch and withers; and the branches are gathered, thrown into the fire, and burned.' Here we encounter Jesus' famous parable of the vine and the branches. Only those who abide in Jesus will bear fruit, for 'apart from me you can do nothing' (John 15:5). Not abiding in Jesus has severe consequences, for those who do not abide are cast away and wither up and die. Then the dead branches are collected, cast into the fire and burned. Certainly we must take into account that Jesus tells a parable here, and it is well known that it is dangerous to press details in parables too far. On the other hand, it seems that the point of verse 6 is rather clear. Those who fail to abide in Jesus will be destroyed and burned, signifying a final and irrevocable judgment. The language used excludes the notion that those in question merely lose their rewards. Moreover, the words are addressed to Jesus' disciples, for verse 2 says that 'Every branch in me that does not bear fruit he takes away.' The phrase 'every branch in me' designates at the very least those who claimed to be Jesus' disciples.

## Warnings in Paul

Numerous texts could be selected in Paul in which he admonishes his readers, cautioning them about the danger of falling away from the gospel. For space reasons I restrict myself to three: Gal. 5:2–4, Rom. 11:19–22, and 1 Cor. 6:9–11. We begin with Gal. 5:2–4. Galatians is directed to those who were tempted to submit to circumcision in order to become part of the family of Abraham. Paul argues vigorously in the letter that taking such a step repudiates the cross of Christ and the new age that has been inaugurated (cf. Gal. 1:4; 2:21; 3:1, 13; 4:4–5; 5:11; 6:12, 14–15, 17). One of his most dramatic warnings is found in Gal. 5:2–4. 'Look: I, Paul, say to you that if you accept circumcision, Christ will be of no advantage to you. I testify again to every man who accepts circumcision that he is obligated to keep the whole law. You are severed from Christ, you who would be justified by the law; you have fallen away from grace.' Stark alternatives are posed here between law and grace, between circumcision and Christ. We need to see here that the admonition is prospective, for Paul counsels the Galatians as they contemplate whether they should be circumcised. Paul does not upbraid them for accepting circumcision but warns them of the consequences of receiving it. The 'if' in verse 2 clarifies that we have a warning here instead of a pronouncement. Hence the aorist verbs in verse 4 should not be read to signify an already existing reality. The statements in verse 4 must be read to cohere with the context as a whole, so that the Galatians will be 'severed from Christ' and will fall 'from grace' *if* they submit to circumcision.[6] Therefore, the text should be understood as a prospective warning, not as a curse or pronouncement on those who have already been circumcised.

We must note carefully the threat that is directed against those who receive circumcision. Christ will no longer profit them (v. 2). Paul does not merely mean that they will lose their rewards but are still assured of eternal life. If they submit to circumcision,

---

6. The aorist verbs 'severed' (*katērgēthēte*) and 'have fallen' (*exepesate*) in
   Gal. 5:4 have a gnomic sense. See also J. B. Lightfoot, *The Epistle of St.
   Paul to the Galatians with Introductions, Notes and Dissertations* (reprint;
   Grand Rapids: Zondervan, 1957), p. 204. Bruce takes them as prolep-
   tic aorists, which leads to the same conclusion. See F. F. Bruce, *The
   Epistle to the Galatians: A Commentary on the Greek Text* (NIGTC; Grand
   Rapids: Eerdmans, 1982), p. 231. Richard N. Longenecker's explanation
   is awkward. He reads the aorist verbs as designating the past and the
   present tense verb (*dikaiousthe*) as denoting the present: *Galatians* (WBC;
   Dallas: Word, 1990), p. 228. A more satisfactory understanding of verbal
   aspect recognizes that verbs should be construed in light of aspect rather
   than time. Whether aorist verbs denote past time must be discerned in
   context, and the context here shows that past time is not in view.

they have no hope of eschatological salvation.[7] Indeed, they are required to keep the whole law to obtain salvation, if they place themselves under the law by accepting circumcision (v. 3). Returning to the law is fatal, however, because perfect obedience is demanded (see Gal. 3:10).[8] Nor can anyone look to the Sinai covenant for forgiveness any longer, for now that Christ has come atonement is available only through the cross. If OT sacrifices provide forgiveness for sins, then Christ died for nothing (Gal. 2:21). Hence, if the Galatians reverted to the Sinai covenant, they would be compelled to keep the law perfectly, since the provisions for forgiveness under that covenant are now cancelled. The OT sacrifices, in other words, point typologically to Christ's sacrifice, and now that the latter has arrived the former are superfluous.

Verse 4 conclusively shows that the result of accepting circumcision is eschatological destruction. Those who submit to circumcision 'are severed' from Christ. Instead of being justified by Christ they are attempting to be justified via the law. Justification by observance of the law, according to Paul, is impossible. Therefore, those who look to the Sinai covenant and the law for salvation by being circumcised 'have fallen away from grace'. To fall away from grace is to be cut off from Christ. Paul does not say, therefore, to the Galatian believers: 'Now that you are believers, you are eschatologically secure no matter what you do.' Rather, he warns them that if they accept circumcision in order to gain salvation they will be cut off from Christ and will be outside the realm of grace.

---

7. Rightly, Hans Dieter Betz, *Galatians: A Commentary on Paul's Letter to the Churches in Galatia* (Hermeneia; Philadelphia: Fortress, 1979), p. 259.

8. This reading of Gal. 3:10 is controversial. For a defence, see Thomas R. Schreiner, 'Is Perfect Obedience to the Law Possible? A Re-examination of Galatians 3:10', *JETS* 27 (1984), pp. 151-160; idem, 'Paul and Perfect Obedience to the Law: An Evaluation of the View of E. P. Sanders', *WTJ* 47 (1985), pp. 245–278.

Another remarkable warning in Paul is found in Rom. 11:19–22. Paul is in the midst of a complex argument in Romans 9–11 where he defends God's faithfulness to the Jewish people. The illustration of the olive tree is taken up in Rom. 11:17–24. Paul remarks that many of the original Jewish branches were removed and instead 'unnatural' branches from the Gentiles were grafted onto the olive tree (the people of God). Paul fears that the Gentiles' ingrafting onto the olive tree will lead to arrogance on their part. Hence he warns them in Rom. 11:19–22:

> Then you will say, 'Branches were broken off so that I might be grafted in.' That is true. They were broken off because of their unbelief, but you stand fast through faith. So do not become proud, but fear. For if God did not spare the natural branches, neither will he spare you. Note then the kindness and the severity of God: severity toward those who have fallen, but God's kindness to you, provided you continue in his kindness. Otherwise you too will be cut off.

Many of the Jews were severed from the olive tree so that the Gentiles could be grafted onto the olive tree. But the Jews were cut off from the people of God because of their failure to believe, and the Gentiles only continue to be part of the olive tree because of their faith. Hence, if they abandon their faith, they also will be detached from the olive tree. A reverent fear should characterize their lives rather than pride, since they retain a place in the olive tree only by virtue of God's kindness. Further, they must also remember God's severity. For if they do not persist in faith, they will also be removed from the olive tree.[9]

---

9. John Calvin minimizes the warning by considering whether it is addressed to the elect: *The Epistles of Paul the Apostle to the Romans and to the Thessalonians*, trans. by R. MacKenzie, ed. by D. W. Torrance and T. F. Torrance (Calvin's Commentaries; Grand Rapids: Eerdmans, 1960), pp. 250–253. But he also, rightly, says: 'It is not enough to have embraced

The nature of the warning seems clear. The Jews removed from the olive tree do not belong to the people of God, and unless they put their faith in Christ they will not enjoy eschatological salvation. Hence, when Paul says to the believing Gentiles that they 'will be cut off' if they do not 'stand fast through faith', he means that they will be cut off from the olive tree just as the Jews were removed. Hence detachment from the olive tree surely represents separation from the people of God. Those who refuse to continue in faith will not enjoy God's kindness but suffer his severity. Unless they repent, their destination will be eternal destruction instead of eternal life.

The last Pauline warning we shall investigate is 1 Cor. 6:9–11. This warning follows on the heels of a rebuke given to the Corinthians for the lawsuits among themselves that they could not resolve. Instead of sacrificing for the sake of fellow believers, they were cheating and defrauding one another. The close link between 1 Cor. 6:1–8 and 6:9–11 is obscured by most versions, though the NRSV captures it well. Verse 8 indicts the Corinthians for their behaviour in the lawsuits: 'You yourselves wrong (*adikeite*) and defraud.' The warning follows in v. 9: 'Do you not know that wrongdoers (*adikoi*) will not inherit the kingdom of God?' The link in the *adik-* words demonstrates that the warning is addressed to the same persons engaged in the lawsuits.[10] Therefore, it follows that the warning is addressed to the believing community in Corinth, and verses 9–11 are not directed to unbelievers.

The warning in 1 Cor. 6:9–11, which follows verse 8, is addressed to believers.

> Or do you not know that the unrighteous will not inherit the kingdom
> of God? Do not be deceived: neither the sexually immoral, nor

---

only once the grace of God, unless during the whole course of your life you follow his call' (p. 252).

10. Gordon D. Fee rightly detects the connection: *The First Epistle to the Corinthians* (NICNT; Grand Rapids: Eerdmans, 1987), p. 242.

idolaters, nor adulterers, nor men who practise homosexuality, nor thieves, nor the greedy, nor drunkards, nor revilers, nor swindlers will inherit the kingdom of God. And such were some of you. But you were washed, you were sanctified, you were justified in the name of the Lord Jesus Christ and by the Spirit of our God.

The content of the warning is not terribly difficult to discern. Not inheriting the kingdom means that the unrighteous will not obtain eternal life (cf. Gal. 5:21; Eph. 5:5). Elsewhere Paul argues that believers who suffer and endure are worthy of entrance into the kingdom (2 Thess. 1:5). That entering the kingdom involves eschatological salvation is clear from Paul's confidence about his future, stated in 2 Tim. 4:18: 'The Lord . . . will save me into his heavenly kingdom.'[11] Those who give themselves over to unrighteousness will not enjoy end-time salvation, but will face God's judgment. Paul emphasizes in 1 Cor. 6:9–11 that such behaviour is not fitting for those who have new life in Christ and are washed, sanctified, and justified. The Corinthians must live in accord with their calling, and if they devote themselves to evil, then judgment will be their destiny.

Jonathan Edwards rightly describes the function of the warnings in a sermon preached on Phil. 3:17:

Here you see the apostle is very careful lest he should be a castaway, and denies his carnal appetites, and mortifies his flesh, for that reason. He did not say, 'I am safe, I am sure I shall never be lost; why need I take any further care respecting it?' Many think because they suppose themselves converted, and so safe, that they have nothing to do with the awful threatenings of God's word, and those terrible denunciations of damnation that are contained in it. When they hear them, they hear them as things which belong only to others, and not at all to themselves, as though there were no application of what is revealed in the Scripture respecting hell, to the godly. And therefore, when

11. The translation here is my own.

they hear awakening sermons about the awful things that God has threatened to the wicked, they do not hear them for themselves, but only for others. But it was not thus with this holy apostle, who certainly was as safe from hell, and as far from a damnable state, as any of us. He looked upon himself as still nearly concerned in God's threatenings of eternal damnation, notwithstanding all his hope, and all his eminent holiness, and therefore gave great diligence, that he might avoid eternal damnation. For he considered that eternal misery was as certainly connected with a wicked life as ever it was, and that it was absolutely necessary that he should still keep under his body, and bring it into subjection, in order that he might not be damned; because indulging the lusts of the body and being damned were more surely connected together. The apostle knew that this conditional proposition was true concerning him, as ever it was. 'If I live wickedly, or do not live in a way of universal obedience to God's commands, I shall certainly be a castaway.' This is evident, because the apostle mentions a proposition of this nature concerning himself in that very chapter where he says, he kept under his body lest he should be a castaway. 1 Cor. ix. 16. 'For though I preach the gospel, I have nothing to glory of, for necessity is laid upon me; yea, woe is unto me if I preach not the gospel.' What necessity was there upon the apostle to preach the gospel, though God had commanded him, for he was already converted, and was safe; and if he had neglected to preach the gospel, how could he have perished after he was converted? But yet this conditional proposition was still true; if he did not live a life of obedience to God, woe would be to him; woe to him, if he did not preach the gospel. The connexion still held. It is impossible a man should go any where else than to hell in a way of disobedience to God. And therefore he deemed it necessary for him to preach the gospel on that account, and on the same account he deemed it necessary to keep under his body, lest he should be a castaway.[12]

---

12. From the sermon 'The Character of Paul an Example to Christians', accessed at http://www.biblebb.com/files/edwards/paul.htm on 10 June 2008.

As noted previously, many other texts from Paul could be introduced here (cf. Rom. 8:13; 1 Cor. 9:24 – 10:13; 15:1–2; 16:22; Gal. 5:19–21; 6:8–9; Eph. 5:5–6; Col. 1:21–23; 3:5–6; 1 Thess. 4:3–8; 2 Tim. 2:11–18). The texts selected indicate that Paul warns believers about the severe consequences of unbelief and disobedience. Moreover, the consequence threatened is eternal destruction, not merely the loss of fruitfulness in this life or extra rewards in the next.

## 2 Peter

Peter exhorts his readers in his second letter about the need for perseverance.[13] False teachers, who apparently espoused libertinism, endangered the church with their so-called path to freedom.[14] Peter's aim in the letter was to dissuade his readers from deviating from the way of the gospel. In 2 Pet. 1:5–11 we see a rather lengthy exhortation:

> For this very reason, make every effort to supplement your faith with virtue, and virtue with knowledge, and knowledge with self-control, and self-control with steadfastness, and steadfastness with godliness, and godliness with brotherly affection, and brotherly affection with love. For if these qualities are yours and are increasing, they keep you from being ineffective or unfruitful in the knowledge of our Lord Jesus Christ. For whoever lacks these qualities is so nearsighted that he is blind, having forgotten that he was cleansed from his former sins. Therefore, brothers, be all the more diligent to make your calling and election sure, for if you practise these qualities you will never fall. For in this way there will be richly provided for you an entrance into the eternal kingdom of our Lord and Saviour Jesus Christ.

---

13. In support of Petrine authorship, see Thomas R. Schreiner, *1, 2 Peter, Jude* (NAC; Nashville: Broadman Holman, 2003), pp. 255–276.
14. For the opponents in 2 Peter, see Schreiner, *1, 2 Peter, Jude*, pp. 277–280.

In verses 5–7 the readers are exhorted to practise the virtues outlined, but Peter does not fall prey to works-righteousness here. All the virtues are the result of faith (v. 5), and they are also the consequence of divine power (vv. 3–4) working in believers' lives.[15]

It seems incontrovertible that Peter addresses believers here, since in verse 1 he addresses 'those who have obtained a faith of equal standing with ours', and the subject remains the same in verses 5–11. What motivation is given to the readers for pursuing these virtues? In verse 8, those who abound in these qualities are fruitful. Those abandoning such virtues are blinded, so that they have forgotten the forgiveness of their sins (v. 9). Practising these virtues is necessary to ensure one's calling and election (v. 10). The references to calling and election indicate that the qualities in verses 5–7 are necessary for eschatological salvation. Hence the 'entrance' into the kingdom in verse 11 does not refer to rewards above and beyond eternal life, but reception into the kingdom itself.[16] Such a reading fits with the whole of 2 Peter, for the false teachers and their followers are clearly destined for final judgment (see 2 Pet. 2:1–3, 20–22). Hence in 2 Pet. 1:8–11 a reference to eschatological salvation accords with the entire message of 2 Peter.[17]

---

15. For the foundational character of 2 Pet 1:3–4, see J. M. Starr, *Sharers in Divine Nature: 2 Peter 1:4 in its Hellenistic Context* (ConBNT 33; Stockholm: Almqvist & Wiksell, 2000), pp. 24–26; J. H. Neyrey, *2 Peter, Jude* (AB; Garden City: Doubleday, 1993), p. 150; J. D. Charles, *Virtue amidst Vice: The Catalog of Virtues in 2 Peter 1* (JSNTSup 150; Sheffield: Sheffield Academic Press, 1997), p. 84.

16. See here the comments of Charles in *Virtue amidst Vice*, p. 152.

17. A similar argument could be made from Jude, since it matches 2 Peter so closely.

## 2 John

This letter of John is remarkably brief and seems to address some of the same matters that concern 1 John. Most commentators are probably correct in identifying the elect lady in 2 John as the church, and the children to refer to the members of the church.[18] The verses that relate to the theme investigated here are 2 John 7–8: 'For many deceivers have gone out into the world, those who do not confess the coming of Jesus Christ in the flesh. Such a one is the deceiver and the antichrist. Watch yourselves, so that you may not lose what we have worked for, but may win a full reward.' Verse 7 is directed against docetists, who denied that Jesus as the Christ came as a human being.[19] Itinerants bearing this message are characterized as deceivers and antichrists (cf. 1 John 2:18–27). Obviously John does not think they are authentic Christians. In verse 8, however, he addresses the church, warning them against losing what they have worked for, so that they may obtain the 'full reward'. Some may think that John refers to a reward above and beyond eternal life, since he speaks of the fullness of the reward. This case seems even more convincing to some who think eternal life is irrevocable, since John speaks of 'losing what they have worked for', and it is argued that none can 'lose' eternal life. Despite the cogency of such arguments, it is more likely that John warns his readers against losing eternal life.[20] The context refers to deceivers and antichrists who have a seriously deficient Christology. John does not think their error is insignificant, but

---

18. So John R. W. Stott, *The Epistles of John* (TNTC; Grand Rapids: Eerdmans, 1964), pp. 200–202; Raymond E. Brown, *The Epistles of John* (AB; Garden City: Doubleday, 1982), pp. 651–655; Stephen S. Smalley, *1, 2, 3 John* (WBC; Waco, TX: Word, 1984), p. 318.

19. Cf. here Smalley, *1, 2, 3 John*, pp. 222–223.

20. Rightly, Brown, *The Epistles of John*, pp. 686–687; Smalley, *1, 2, 3 John*, pp. 330–332.

damning, according to verse 7. Moreover, verse 9 immediately follows the warning in verse 8, and it shows that eternal life is in view. Those who 'progress' and do not continue in orthodox teaching do not have God. Conversely, those who continue in the faith have 'both the Father and the Son'. Deviation from the teaching here has ultimate consequences, since those who are unfaithful do not even 'have' (echō) God. Given that verse 8 is folded between verses 7 and 9 and these verses have to do with whether one belongs to God, the warning in verse 8 should be understood as referring to eternal life.

## Warnings in Revelation

Revelation is addressed to churches suffering persecution from the beast, which is almost certainly the Roman empire. John calls on believers to endure the blandishments of the beast and the false prophets, knowing that evil will ultimately be judged and the righteous will be rewarded. We are not surprised to learn, then, that warnings and exhortations permeate the book. We will confine ourselves, for the sake of brevity, to the exhortations given to the seven churches. In every letter, believers are urged to overcome or conquer in order to obtain the reward (Rev. 2:7, 11, 17, 26; 3:5, 12, 21). Nor do we need to investigate every one of these exhortations in detail, for they all have the same function. Therefore, if the nature of the exhortations in Revelation 2–3 can be determined, it should be clear whether these texts function in the same way as the other warning passages previously considered.

The exhortations are given to the churches in Revelation 2–3. This is clear from the refrain, 'He who has an ear, let him hear what the Spirit says to the churches' (Rev. 2:7, 11, 17, 29; 3:6, 13, 22). John urges the readers to 'conquer' near the conclusion of each of the seven letters (Rev. 2:7, 11, 17, 26; 3:5, 12, 21). The crucial question for our purposes is to discern why believers must overcome and conquer. In other words, what will they lose if they fail to conquer? Revelation 2:11 provides a clear answer: 'The one who conquers will not be hurt by the second death.' The 'second death' doubtless refers to final judgment, for in Rev. 20:14 John writes, 'This is the second death, the lake of fire' (cf. also Rev. 20:6; 21:8). Indeed, the next verse affirms that 'if anyone's name was not found written in the book of life, he was thrown into the lake of fire' (Rev. 20:15). The call to conquer, then, is not a minor matter, for it is necessary to escape eternal judgment in the lake of fire. Conversely, those who do not conquer will find that their destiny is the lake of fire, for they will die the second death.

When we consider the remaining exhortations to conquer, there are good reasons to conclude that conquering is necessary to obtain eternal life.[21] We would expect such a conclusion, for it would be quite surprising if the conquering texts promised distinct rewards. It is well known in scholarship that the letters to the seven churches contain the same basic elements, though some differences emerge among the letters. Still, there is no reason to think that the conquering texts function in a remarkably different way in the various letters. That is, it seems that in each letter one must conquer to obtain eternal life. For instance, only those who conquer 'will eat of the tree of life, which is in the paradise of God' (Rev. 2:7). Only those who eat of the tree of life are in the holy city, the new Jerusalem (Rev. 22:2, 14, 19). Hence, it follows that the tree of life also describes eternal life. In the same way, 'the hidden manna' and the 'white stone' designate entrance into the company of God's people (Rev. 2:17).[22] The rule over the nations is not a reward above and beyond eternal life (Rev. 2:26). Instead, it is the promise for every person who belongs to God and

---

21. Cf. here Richard Bauckham, *The Theology of the Book of Revelation* (Cambridge: Cambridge University Press, 1993), p. 14.

22. See G. K. Beale, *The Book of Revelation* (NIGTC; Grand Rapids: Eerdmans, 1999), p. 252.

conquers. Those who conquer wear 'white garments', signalling worthiness to enter God's presence (Rev. 3:5). That the reward is eternal life is instantly clarified by John, for those who wear such garments will not be erased from 'the book of life' (Rev. 3:5). Jesus himself will acknowledge before the Father and angels that such persons belong to him (cf. Matt 10:32). The overcomer will be 'a pillar in the temple of my God' (Rev. 3:12). In other words, as the verse goes on to show, such a person will be part of the new Jerusalem and will have God's name imprinted on him. So, too, the one who conquers will reign with Jesus on his throne (Rev. 3:21). Yes, this is a stunning reward, but it is one promised to all believers, to all who conquer.

To sum up, in Revelation John addresses believers facing discrimination and persecution. He exhorts them to persevere, to continue in faith, and to overcome and conquer. These exhortations do not address minor matters, for only those who conquer will enter paradise and avoid the second death. Hence, overcoming is a condition that must be met for one to enjoy eternal life.

## Warnings in Hebrews

I am considering the warnings in Hebrews last because they often dominate the discussion. The thesis defended here is that the warnings in Hebrews function in the same way as most of the other warnings found in the NT. More specifically, the warnings in Hebrews accord with the other warnings presented in this chapter. Hence the warnings in Hebrews, though they are quite remarkable, given the intensity of the language, are not dramatically different from the other warning texts already examined. I will try to defend this view in the brief discussion that follows.

One of the crucial truths that must be noted in interpreting the warning passages in Hebrews is that the admonitions must be read together. This observation is one of the crucial insights in

Scot McKnight's important essay on these texts in Hebrews.[23] The letter to the Hebrews is a sermon sent to the church (Heb. 13:22), and hence it should not be interpreted primarily as a theological treatise. The warnings that punctuate the letter all serve the same purpose. The writer does not admonish the readers repeatedly as if he has several different ends in view. The warnings should be read synoptically, and hence the warnings are mutually illuminating. Many scholars have made the mistake, for instance, of isolating Hebrews 6 from the other warning texts, so that they sink their energies into reading Hebrews 6 alone. Or they inadvertently start reading the warning of Hebrews 6 as if it represents a defection that has already taken place.[24] It is not my intention to defend in detail here the interpretation proposed for the warning texts in Hebrews. I hope to show that reading the warnings synoptically helps us understand to whom they are addressed and their function. The warning passages in Hebrews are identified

---

23. McKnight, 'The Warning Passages in Hebrews', pp. 21–59.

24. E.g., Osborne fails to grasp this point when he insists that the participle 'fall away' (*parapesontas*) cannot be conditional ('A Classical Arminian View', pp. 112, 114, 116). In drawing this conclusion Osborne turns this text against the other warning passages in Hebrews, so that Hebrews 6 makes a declaration about those who have fallen away, while the other warning passages warn the readers from falling away. It is quite improbable, though, that the author is both warning the readers against falling away in some passages and declaring that some have already fallen away in others. Hebrews 6 should be read in the same way as the other exhortations in Hebrews: as a warning. The assurance the author offers the readers in Heb. 6:9 seems to confirm that the text functions as a warning, for the readers who are assured in verse 9 are the same ones who are warned in the previous verses. Significantly, Cockerill, who agrees with Osborne's overall reading, differs from Osborne on this point, rightly seeing that Heb. 6:6 is conditional ('A Wesleyan Arminian View', pp. 275–276).

here as Heb. 2:1–4; 3:12 – 4:13; 5:11 – 6:12; 10:19–39; 12:25–29. Even though scholars may disagree over the exact range of the warning texts in Hebrews, the case made here does not depend upon a precise delimitation of the admonitions.

Three issues must be resolved in the warning texts in Hebrews. First, to whom are the warnings addressed? Second, what is the nature or character of the warning? Third, what is the consequence of failing to heed the warning? The questions will be taken up in order, and they will be answered by taking into account all the warning texts in the letter. We begin, then, by asking to whom the warnings are addressed. It seems clear that the warnings are addressed to believers. In the first warning, in Heb. 2:1–4, the author says that 'we must pay much closer attention to what we have heard, lest we drift away from it' (v. 1). The first person plurals indicate that the author includes himself in those who need to hear his admonition. Apparently, the warning is intended for all believers. The second warning, in Heb. 3:12 – 4:13, has the same character. The writer addresses 'brothers', admonishing them to beware 'lest there be in any of you an evil, unbelieving heart, leading you to fall away from the living God' (3:12). The word 'brothers' refers to the believing community, and he directs his words in the second person plural to believers so that they will enjoy God's eschatological rest (cf. also v. 13). In verse 14, however, the writer shifts to the first person plural, so that he again includes himself in the admonition: 'For we have come to share in Christ, if indeed we hold our original confidence firm to the end.' That the text is directed to believers is evident from the remainder of the warning. In verse 4:1 both the first person and second person plural are included. 'Let us fear, lest any of you should seem to have failed to reach' God's rest. The writer concludes with the words, 'let us therefore strive to enter that rest' (v. 11).

Because of the controversy over Hebrews 6, we shall leave that passage to the end and examine Heb. 10:26–31 and 12:25–29 first. The warning in Heb. 10:26–31 begins with the words 'For if we go on sinning deliberately after receiving knowledge of the truth, there no longer remains a sacrifice for sins' (v. 26). Again, the writer includes himself in the warning, demonstrating that the admonition is intended for believers. In the final warning in Heb. 12:25 the writer uses the second person plural: 'See that you do not refuse him who is speaking.' Again, it is evident that the admonition is for believers. The same pattern is clear in Heb. 5:11 – 6:12. The writer begins with 'you' when he indicts the readers for their sluggishness and dullness. He commences the exhortation, however, with the first person plural, 'let us . . . go on to maturity' (Heb. 6:1). Note the first person plural in Heb. 6:3 as well.

What I have argued for thus far may seem rather prosaic and obvious. The admonitions are directed to believers. Still, Fanning may be correct in suggesting that the use of 'we' and 'you' is for pastoral reasons and does not settle the issue.[25] Scholars have invested much energy in determining the referents of 'those who have once been enlightened, who have tasted the heavenly gift, and have shared in the Holy Spirit, and have tasted the goodness of the word of God and the powers of the age to come'. We can understand why this is so, for here the writer identifies in detail the spiritual condition of the readers. It is most natural to conclude that the writer refers to believers. The decisive evidence for this conclusion is that the author says they are partakers of the

---

25. Fanning, 'A Classical Reformed View', p. 180. Though Fanning remarks that 'a straightforward reading of these descriptions leads us to understand them to refer to full and genuine Christian experience' (p. 180), he concludes at the end of his essay that Heb. 6:4–5 portrays 'the *phenomena* of their conversion, what their Christian experience looked like outwardly. He portrays them in distinctly Christian terms to emphasize how close they have been to the faith and what they are rejecting if they depart' (p. 217). Hence, at the end of the day, Fanning argues that the descriptions in Heb. 6:4–5 do not necessarily refer to true believers, only to those who appeared to be believers.

Holy Spirit. Having the Spirit is the *sine qua non* of what it means to be a Christian (cf. Gal. 3:1–5; Acts 15:7–11).[26] Nor can the word 'partakers' (*metochous*) be restricted to superficial experiences of the Spirit. Just a few verses earlier the verbal form of the word is used for 'everyone who partakes [*metechōn*] only of milk' (Heb. 5:13). Obviously the writer refers to the full ingestion of milk, not to merely sipping it. In the same way, he describes the readers as those who have received the Holy Spirit.

Many seem to be unaware that Charles Spurgeon identified the readers in view in Hebrews 6 as believers. He remarks:

> First, then, we answer the question, WHO ARE THE PEOPLE HERE SPOKEN OF? If you read Dr. Gill, Dr. Owen, and almost all the eminent Calvinistic writers, they all of them assert that these persons are not Christians. They say, that enough is said here to represent a man who is a Christian externally, but not enough to give the portrait of a true believer. Now, it strikes me they would not have said this if they had had some doctrine to uphold; for a child, reading this passage, would say, that *the persons intended by it must be Christians.* If the Holy Spirit intended to describe Christians, I do not see that he could have used more explicit terms than there are here. How can a man be said to be enlightened, and to taste of the heavenly gift, and to be made partaker of the Holy Ghost, without being a child of God? With all deference to these learned doctors, and I admire and love them all, I humbly conceive that they allowed their judgments to be a little warped when they said that; and I think I shall be able to show that none but true believers are here described.[27]

---

26. Cf. Osborne, 'A Classical Arminian View', p. 114; Cockerill, 'A Wesleyan Arminian View', pp. 273–274.

27. Charles Spurgeon's sermon on Heb. 6:4–6 ('Final Perseverance', in *The New Park Street Pulpit*, accessed on 3 June 2008 at http://www.spurgeon. org/sermons/0075.htm).

The most natural reading of Hebrews 6, then, is to see the writer as addressing the same audience addressed in the other admonitions in the letter. To put it another way, the warning in Hebrews 6 is not a judgment on the spiritual state of those addressed. That is, the writer is not subtly implying that they have had many genuine experiences but they are not genuinely Christians.[28] Rather, he warns them about the consequence of falling away even though they have received great privileges. To sum up: all the evidence in Hebrews suggests that the warnings are addressed to believers. To read Hebrews 6 as containing a different kind of warning constitutes a failure to read the warnings synoptically and also misreads the specific descriptions of the readers in Heb. 6:4–5.[29]

The second question relates to the nature or character of the warnings. Again the texts will be interpreted synoptically, so that when read mutually the richness and depth of the admonitions can be gleaned. First of all, the readers are warned against drifting away (Heb. 2:1) or neglecting their salvation (Heb. 2:3). In Hebrews 3 they are warned against hardening their hearts (Heb. 3:7–8, 15), and the wilderness generation is indicted for going astray in their hearts (Heb. 3:10). 'An evil, unbelieving heart' leads one to 'fall away from the living God' (Heb. 3:12). Hence, the readers must not become stubborn, so that they are 'hardened by

---

28. Fanning objects to the view proposed by Caneday and me, arguing that he sees the warnings as prospective as well ('A Classical Reformed View', p. 218, n. 99). But our views still differ, because he specifically identifies those described in Heb. 6:4–5 as those who appear to be Christians (p. 217).

29. Note how the readers are described as 'sanctified' in Heb. 10:29. The term here does not merely refer to outward cleansing (against Grudem, 'Perseverance of the Saints', pp. 177–178), nor is the language merely phenomenological (against Fanning, 'A Classical Reformed View', p. 217). It most naturally refers to those sanctified by the work of Jesus Christ on the cross, which is a major theme in Hebrews.

the deceitfulness of sin' (Heb. 3:13). They are encouraged to continue to hold onto Christ (Heb. 3:14). They must not be like the wilderness generation that did not enter God's rest because they 'rebelled' (Heb. 3:16), 'sinned' (Heb. 3:17), and failed to obey and believe (Heb. 3:18–19). Hence, the readers must labour to enter God's rest (Heb. 4:11).[30]

In Heb. 6:1 the readers are urged to become mature. In verse 6 the writer warns them against falling away. Some understand the participle here (*parapesontas*), given the use of the preceding participles in verses 4–5, to say that the readers have already fallen away. Such a reading, however, does not fit with all the other admonitions in Hebrews, for the author does not chide the readers because they have fallen away but admonishes them so that they will not fall away. Indeed, the context of chapter 6 fits such an interpretation as well. The readers are urged to diligence and to refrain from dullness, so that they will possess the promises (vv. 11–12). They are encouraged to lay hold of the future hope of realizing the eschatological inheritance (v. 18).

---

30. Gleason makes the mistake of inverting the warning passages in Hebrews, so that he reads them through the lenses of the fall of Israel in the wilderness ('A Moderate Reformed View', pp. 322–377). What he fails to see, however, is the nature of biblical typology. The physical destruction of Israel becomes a type of *eternal* and *eschatological* judgment. In other words, typology is characterized by escalation. Hence, the physical judgment of Sodom and Gomorrah functions as a type of final judgment (cf. 2 Pet. 2:6, 9; Jude 7). For this critique of Gleason, see Osborne, 'A Classical Arminian View', pp. 384–390; Fanning, 'A Classical Reformed View', pp. 406–410. Furthermore, against Gleason, it is scarcely clear that the judgment threatened in Hebrews can be identified as the destruction of Palestine and Jerusalem in AD 66–70 (rightly, Osborne, 'A Classical Arminian View', pp. 392–393; Fanning, 'A Classical Reformed View', pp. 403–406; Cockerill, 'A Wesleyan Arminian View', pp. 418–419).

The warnings are prospective. The author does not cast a glance backward retrospectively and indict them because they have fallen away. He admonishes them lest their sluggishness will lead them to fall away.

In chapter 10 the recipients are exhorted to draw near (v. 22), to hold on to the confession (v. 23), to reflect on how they can stimulate one another to godliness (vv. 24–25). They must not deliberately turn their backs on Christ's sacrifice and deny the only sacrifice that atones for sin (v. 26). The readers must not abandon their confidence but endure and not shrink back (vv. 35–39). The call to persevere is nothing other than a call to faith (so Hebrews 11). Finally, in Heb. 12:25 the readers are warned not to 'refuse him who is speaking'.

The admonitions in Hebrews are *warnings*. They function prospectively, urging believers not to fall away. In other words, they admonish the readers not to commit apostasy and to fall away from Jesus Christ. The writer's aim is not to counsel believers against sin. Rather, he admonishes them not to commit apostasy. The author, of course, does not take any sin lightly, but what he warns against is final and definitive rejection of Jesus Christ. That is why he says there is no sacrifice that can be offered for those who have rejected Christ's atonement (Heb. 10:26).[31] The sin envisioned is not a temporary lapse but represents a re-crucifixion of the Son of God (Heb. 6:6), which is unthinkable and represents forsaking Jesus. The language of refusing and rejecting points

---

31. Against Gleason, 'A Moderate Reformed View', pp. 358–359. If no
    sacrifice for sins avails, then there is no forgiveness for those who sin
    wilfully. Hence, contra Gleason, the punishment cannot be restricted
    to physical death. As Philip E. Hughes says, 'to reject this sacrifice is to
    be left with no sacrifice at all': *A Commentary on the Epistle to the Hebrews*
    (Grand Rapids: Eerdmans, 1977), p. 419. So also William L. Lane,
    *Hebrews 9–13* (WBC; Dallas: Word, 1991), p. 293; Harold W. Attridge, *The
    Epistle to the Hebrews* (Hermeneia; Philadelphia: Fortress, 1989), p. 293.

to the same reality (Heb. 12:25). Apostasy is clearly in view, when the author speaks of trampling Jesus as God's Son under one's feet, of considering the blood of the covenant to be unclean, and of insulting the Spirit who grants grace (Heb. 10:29). Without minimizing any sin, the author does not refer to the sins that plague Christians daily. Apostasy slams the door shut against the Christian gospel and turns to something or someone else for a source of life. The author of Hebrews, then, does not accuse his readers of *already* committing apostasy. He warns them most severely about the consequences of moving in such a direction.

This brings us to the third issue in the warning texts: the consequences that will follow if the readers do not heed the warning. Those who drift away will not escape God's judgment if they forsake him (Heb. 2:3). They shall never enter God's eschatological rest if they harden their hearts in unbelief (Heb. 3:11, 18; 4:3, 5, 11). They cannot be renewed again to repentance (6:6). If they fall away the day of eschatological cursing is near, and the final outcome will be burning (6:7–8). No atonement or sacrifice for sins will avail for them, since they have repudiated Christ's atonement for them (10:26). All that lies in store for them is terrifying judgment and God's fire that will consume his adversaries (10:27). Their destiny will be God's punishment and vengeance on the day the Lord judges his own (10:29–30). God will not delight in them but instead he will destroy them, since they did not continue in faith (10:38–39). The word for 'destruction' (*apōleia*) is a typical term in the NT for eschatological punishment of the wicked (cf. Matt. 7:13; John 17:12; Acts 8:20; Rom. 9:22; Phil. 1:28; 3:19; 2 Thess. 2:3; 1 Tim. 6:9; 2 Pet. 2:1, 3; 3:7, 16; Rev. 17:8, 11). Hence there will be no escape (Heb. 12:25) for those who turn away from the author's admonitions.

The consequences of apostasy sketched in above clearly designate end-time punishment, eternal judgment, or final damnation. The language describing the judgment is severe and dramatic, and hence it cannot be restricted to only losing one's reward. Those who forsake Christ will be destroyed for ever, and abandon the only hope they have of forgiveness of sins. The author, therefore, pleads with his readers not to take such a fatal step. He warns them most urgently to cling to Christ and to keep trusting him for the forgiveness of sins and the hope of eternal life.

## Conclusion

I conclude, then, that the warning texts in Hebrews have the same character as the other warning texts we have examined in the NT. They admonish the readers against falling away, for those who do so will be damned forever. It is precisely at this point that we must remind ourselves of the function of the warnings in the NT. The writers in the texts we have examined do not accuse their readers because the latter *have fallen away*. They admonish them *so that they will not fall away*. The warnings are *prospective*, not *retrospective*. They are like road signs that caution drivers of dangers ahead on the highway. They are written so that readers will heed the warnings and escape the consequence threatened. Parents warn their children against running in the street, so that they will not be struck by a car and perish. So too, poisonous products have dramatic signs on them, so no one will ingest the poison and die. The purpose of warnings in the NT is redemptive and salvific. The Lord uses them as means, so that we believers will escape death.

I noted above that Spurgeon believed the warnings in Hebrews were addressed to believers, but he did not conclude that true believers could fall away. He said regarding the warning in Hebrews 6:

> 'But,' says one, 'You say they cannot fall away.' What is the use of putting this 'if' in, like a bugbear to frighten children, or like a ghost that can have no existence? My learned friend, 'Who art thou that repliest against God?' If God has put it in, he has put it in for wise reasons and for excellent purposes. Let me show you why. First, O Christian, it is put in to keep thee from falling away. God preserves

his children from falling away; but he keeps them by the use of means; and one of these is, the terrors of the law, showing them what would happen if they were to fall away. There is a deep precipice: what is the best way to keep any one from going down there? Why, to tell him that if he did he would inevitably be dashed to pieces. In some old castle there is a deep cellar, where there is a vast amount of fixed air and gas, which would kill anybody who went down. What does the guide say? 'If you go down you will never come up alive.' Who thinks of going down? The very fact of the guide telling us what the consequences would be, keeps us from it. Our friend puts away from us a cup of arsenic; he does not want us to drink it, but he says, 'If you drink it, it will kill you.' Does he suppose for a moment that we should drink it? No; he tells us the consequences, and he is sure we will not do it. So God says, 'My child, if you fall over this precipice you will be dashed to pieces.' What does the child do? He says, 'Father, keep me; hold thou me up, and I shall be safe.' It leads the believer to greater dependence on God, to a holy fear and caution, because he knows that if he were to fall away he could not be renewed, and he stands far away from that great gulf, because he knows that if he were to fall into it there would be no salvation for him.[32]

32. Charles Spurgeon's sermon on Heb. 6:4–6 ('Final Perseverance', in *The New Park Street Pulpit*, accessed on 3 June 2008 at http://www.spurgeon. org/sermons/0075.htm).

## 3. PERSEVERING IN FAITH IS NOT PERFECTION

### Introduction

Some who have read the book *The Race Set Before Us* have suggested that it amounts to works-righteousness, or requires a kind of righteousness in the Christian life that few believers attain. I think such criticisms fail to understand the previous book rightly, but in this chapter I would like to clarify further what is intended in saying that believers must run the race to the end in order to be saved. The thesis of the chapter is that persevering in faith is not the same thing as perfection. The warning passages investigated in the last chapter admonish readers against committing apostasy: of falling finally and definitively away from Jesus Christ. They are badly misinterpreted if they are construed to teach that some kind of perfectionism is possible before the day of final redemption.

## Prayers for forgiveness

It was noted previously that warnings permeate the NT writings, but the same writings teach that perfection in this life is not the portion of believers. For instance, the prayer that Jesus taught his disciples includes the request, 'Forgive us our debts, as we also have forgiven our debtors' (Matt. 6:12).[1] The inclusion of this petition in the Lord's Prayer is highly significant. Surely Jesus, in teaching this prayer to his disciples, expected them to voice these requests regularly to God. It is highly improbable that any disciples would come to the point where they could exclude some of the petitions found in the Lord's Prayer. Evidently, then, all disciples continue to sin until the day of their death. Hence, they must humble themselves continually before God and ask him to forgive their sins.

At the same time we must observe another petition in the Lord's Prayer. In the very next verse we are instructed to pray, 'lead us not into temptation, but deliver us from evil' (Matt. 6:13). The focus of this petition is not merely that the Lord would keep believers from sin, though freedom from sin is probably part of it. Still, Jesus particularly has in mind that we would be kept from falling into such temptation that we would fall away from the faith.[2] Deliverance from the evil one here means deliverance from apostasy. If this interpretation is valid, then we have side by side the recognition that believers are imperfect and need to ask for forgiveness of sins every day and a prayer not to commit apostasy. Hence the continued presence of sin in our lives is not the same thing as apostasy. Believers who pray for forgiveness also pray for strength not to fall away. There is regular sin in

---

1. Incidentally, Augustine regularly cites this verse in his controversy with Pelagius.
2. Hagner remarks, 'The petition in this instance concerns severe testing . . . that could eventuate in apostasy': *Matthew 1–13*, p. 151.

believers' lives that cannot be equated with falling away from the Lord.

We see the same kind of truth in 1 John. John insists that all believers continue to sin. Those who claim to be sinless are liars, and the truth of the gospel does not reside in them (1 John 1:8, 10).[3] What it means to be a believer is to 'confess our sins' (1 John 1:9) and to acknowledge the continuing presence of evil in our lives. The 'secessionists' in 1 John have left the church and demonstrated that they did not truly belong to the people of God (1 John 2:19). It is the false teachers, therefore, who claimed to be perfect! And yet they lived antinomian lifestyles at the same time (1 John 1:7; 2:3–6). Here is one of the paradoxes that we find quite often in the NT. Those who claimed perfection had actually given themselves over to evil. Presumably they believed that evil was impossible for them in their exalted spiritual state. Conversely, those who were living in the light and walking in a way that pleased God recognized that sin continued to exist in their lives (1 John 1:7). Indeed, it is as believers walk in the light that they are cleansed of sin, as 1 John 1:7 teaches. The collocation of walking in the light with cleansing from sin indicates that walking in the light cannot be equated with sinlessness. Rather, those who walk in the light are conscious of their continuing imperfection and hence continue to confess their sins. They function in contrast to those who are convinced that they are perfect, so that no confession of sin is necessary.

---

3. I. Howard Marshall argues there is no clear evidence of libertinism in the lifestyle of the opponents: *The Epistles of John* (NICNT; Grand Rapids: Eerdmans, 1978), pp. 14–16. See the discussion in Brown, who argues that the opponents were not Gnostic but indifferent to whether or not they sinned: *The Epistles of John*, pp. 80–83, 234–235.

## Perfection at resurrection

Another crucial text for understanding the biblical perspective on perfection and perseverance is Phil. 3:12–16:

> Not that I have already obtained this or am already perfect, but I press on to make it my own, because Christ Jesus has made me his own. Brothers, I do not consider that I have made it my own. But one thing I do: forgetting what lies behind and straining forward to what lies ahead, I press on toward the goal for the prize of the upward call of God in Christ Jesus. Let those of us who are mature think this way, and if in anything you think otherwise, God will reveal that also to you. Only let us hold true to what we have attained.

The context is illuminating here. Paul warns the Philippians about false teachers, probably Judaizers who advocated circumcision and observance of the Mosaic law for salvation (cf. Phil. 3:2–11). If the standard were righteousness by law, then Paul surpassed them all, for his devotion to the law was extraordinary (Phil. 3:4–6). Nevertheless, the gain that came from being devoted to law-observance and circumcision must be jettisoned to gain Christ and to be found in him (Phil. 3:7–8). Indeed, Paul found righteousness from God only by repudiating his own righteousness that was based on observance of the law (Phil. 3:9). The final declaration of righteousness and the day of resurrection are still future (Phil. 3:9–11). Hence Paul begins verse 12 by stressing that the resurrection is not yet a reality, and hence perfection is not yet his. In Pauline theology, perfection will not be the portion of believers until the day of resurrection. As long as believers inhabit the old age they continue to struggle with sin. They will not be freed completely from the old Adam until the mortal body is raised from the dead. Therefore, those who postulate that the resurrection has already occurred are guilty of an over-realized eschatology

(2 Tim. 2:18).[4] Interestingly, those who claim the resurrection
has already occurred appear to be guilty of the most blatant
kind of antinomianism (cf. 2 Tim. 3:1–5). Perhaps the opponents in 2 Timothy, since they thought they already enjoyed the
life of the resurrection, believed that all their desires accorded
with the life of the age to come. In other words, if believers are
already raised, then all their desires are perfect, and hence the
practice of evil is impossible. It may be that Hymenaeus and
Philetus (2 Tim. 2:17) proposed an argument of this nature.

Even though perfection will only be attained at the resurrection (Phil. 3:11–12), the delay of perfection to the future does not
produce moral laxity in Paul. Paul runs the race with effort and
energy in order to obtain the eschatological prize on the last day.
How he runs the race presently is not severed from the future
reward, even if he does not run perfectly in the present evil age.
Those who are 'mature' or 'perfect' (*teleioi*) know that they cannot
be perfect. They are deeply conscious of their sin, their pride,
their selfishness, their irritability, their pettiness, their anger, and
their lusts. Still, they keep running the race, but not in order to
obtain the reward by works. They run the race in faith, not trusting their own righteousness but looking to Christ for every good
gift. Even if they fail and fall repeatedly, they do not quit the race.
Instead, looking to Christ, they rise again and run to obtain the
prize, trusting in the righteousness of the one who saved them,
not in their own righteousness.

Paul does not claim perfection, since the resurrection is not yet
his (Phil. 3:12). Believers are alive because of the indwelling Spirit,

---

4. The opponents in 2 Tim. perhaps believed that the only resurrection
   believers experienced was spiritual and that it occurred at baptism:
   I. Howard Marshall, in collaboration with Philip H. Towner, *The Pastoral
   Epistles* (ICC; Edinburgh: T. & T. Clark, 1999), pp. 751–754; William D.
   Mounce, *Pastoral Epistles* (WBC; Nashville: Thomas Nelson, 2000), pp.
   527–528.

but their bodies are mortal because of sin (Rom. 8:10).[5] Believers await the promise of the resurrection on the final day (Rom. 8:11). Hence, believers groan with all of creation as they long for the promise of a new creation and as they await the final redemption of their bodies (Rom. 8:19–23). Complete deliverance 'from this body of death' will be realized only at the resurrection (Rom. 7:24). Hence, as long as believers inhabit the already–not yet, they still experience to some degree the struggle with sin depicted in Rom. 7:14–25. They are no longer captives to sin, for they have been freed in Christ Jesus (Rom. 6:6–7, 17–18, 22; 8:2). In union with Christ they have died to sin and been raised to new life (Rom. 6:2–4, 8–10). Subjugation to the flesh, and who believers were in Adam, are things of the past (Rom. 8:12). Still, the resurrection has not yet come, and the mortal body, though not sinful per se, is the continuing emblem of sin until the day believers receive a resurrected body. As long as believers live in mortal bodies, therefore, they will continue to sin and will not obtain perfection.

The progression of thought in Phil. 3:11–12 suggests that perfection will belong to believers on the day when they attain the resurrection, but until then they continue to strive to attain the goal to which God has called them (cf. Phil. 3:14). Believers await the coming of Jesus, who will transform the body so that it is glorious and whole. It seems evident that the struggle with sin will cease at the day of resurrection. We have already seen hints of this elsewhere in Paul. The agonizing battle against sin will end

---

5. Cf. C. E. B. Cranfield, *A Critical and Exegetical Commentary on the Epistle to the Romans: Introduction and Commentary on Romans I-VIII* (ICC; Edinburgh: T. & T. Clark, 1975), p. 389; Douglas J. Moo, *Romans 1–8* (WEC; Chicago: Moody, 1991), pp. 523–524; David Wenham, 'The Christian Life: A Life of Tension? A Consideration of the Nature of Christian Experience in Paul', in D. A. Hagner and M. J. Harris (eds), *Pauline Studies: Essays Presented to Professor F. F. Bruce on his Seventieth Birthday* (Grand Rapids: Eerdmans, 1980), pp. 85–86.

when believers are set free 'from this body of death' (Rom. 7:24).[6]
Believers await the day when their mortal bodies will be raised,
and they will be free from sin (Rom. 8:10–11, 23). Sin and death
entered the world through the first Adam, and conversely righteousness and life have triumphed through the second Adam, Jesus
Christ (Rom. 5:12–19; 1 Cor. 15:21–22). The life of the age to come
has penetrated this evil age, so that in the midst of the present evil
age believers enjoy the life of the age to come and triumph over
sin. Nevertheless, death and sin still exist in believers as long as
the present evil age continues. Complete victory over sin will not
belong to believers until the day of resurrection. Believers groan
as members of the old age until the new age arrives in its fullness
and the day of resurrection dawns (Rom. 8:23; 2 Cor. 5:1–5).

## The exhortations in the epistles

Such a view of perfection matches what we find in all of the NT
epistles. The letters are written to churches in which Christians
continue to battle against sin and to some extent are failing. The
letters are written to call upon believers to live in accord with
their calling. They need to be written because believers in many
instances are not doing the will of God. They are falling short in
many ways, sometimes quite dramatically. The presence of sin in
congregations does not provoke the authors of the epistles to write
off their readers as unbelievers. The readers are warned that if
they abandon Christ or give themselves over to evil, they will face
eschatological judgment. Nowhere is sin tolerated or dismissed as
trivial. On the other hand, the authors do not conclude from the
presence of sin in the churches that the recipients are unbelievers.

---

6. Robert Banks especially emphasizes the future here: 'Romans 7:25a: An
   Eschatological Thanksgiving?' *Australian Biblical Review* 26 (1978), pp.
   39–40.

The writers are not shocked, as if the presence of sin is completely unexpected, or as if it proved that the readers were not believers. It is recognized that the struggle between the flesh and the Spirit is fierce (Gal. 5:17), even if believers can be confident of ultimate victory. The desires of the flesh are incredibly strong, so that they 'wage war against [the] soul' (1 Pet. 2:11).[7] The image of war indicates the incredible strength sinful desires still have in the lives of Christians. Peter does not despair, for believers are not defenceless against such desires; they are able to abstain as those who are born again (1 Pet. 1:3, 23). Still, Christians are not immune from sin or the desires of the flesh.

We see the same truth in Rom. 8:13, where believers by means of the Spirit must 'put to death the deeds of the body'. The metaphor 'put to death' again communicates the attraction of sin in the lives of believers (cf. Col. 3:5). Desires for evil are not passive in believers, but they rise up within them with a strength that can be mastered only when such passions are slain. Naturally no room or excuse is given for sin in the lives of believers, and yet there is an implicit understanding that believers are not outside the realm of sin and do not conquer sin perfectly.[8]

---

7. Martin Luther's comments here are insightful: 'But as soon as the Spirit and faith enter our hearts, we become so weak that we think we cannot beat down the least imaginations and sparks of temptation, and we see nothing but sin in ourselves from the crown of the head even to the foot. For before we believed, we walked according to our own lusts, but now the Spirit has come and would purify us, and a conflict arises when the devil, the flesh, and the world oppose faith.' He goes on to say, 'If thou then hast wicked thoughts, thou shouldst not on this account despair; only be on thy guard, that thou be not taken prisoner by them.' *Commentary on Peter and Jude* (Grand Rapids: Kregel, 1990), pp. 112–113.

8. John Murray says: 'The believer's once-for-all death to the law and to sin does not free him from the necessity of mortifying sin in his members; it makes it *necessary* and *possible* for him to do so': *The Epistle to the Romans:*

## A fascinating remark by James

An aside by James is quite interesting at this point, for it is well
known that James calls upon believers to live in a way that is pleasing to God, and he insists that those who know God show it by
their lives. Faith, as he famously puts it, is dead without works
(cf. Jas. 2:14–26). No one can exempt himself by boasting that he
keeps part of God's law. 'For whoever keeps the whole law but fails
in one point has become accountable for all of it' (Jas. 2:10). The
word translated 'fails' by the ESV here is literally the word 'stumble'
(*ptaiō*). James makes this observation in the middle of an argument
in which he strips away any excuses for partiality. The rigour of
James's ethic shines through the letter on a number of occasions.
And yet in Jas. 3:2, in speaking about the tongue, he remarks, 'we
all stumble in many ways'. The word 'stumble' (*ptaiō*) here is the
same term that was used for 'sin' in Jas. 2:10. No excuses can ever
be offered for sin, and yet James teaches that all Christians without
exception sin. Indeed, he is quite emphatic about this, since he says
'we all' sin.[9] Not only that; all believers stumble 'in many ways'.
Apparently sin is not an occasional lapse in the lives of Christians,
but believers fall short in multiple ways. Here we have confirma-
tion that believers need to keep praying for forgiveness of sins,
since sin still constantly afflicts them. It seems, then, that the call
to godliness in James could be misunderstood as implying a kind
of perfection in the lives of believers, but his comment in Jas. 3:2
reveals that even the most godly believers continue to fall short of
what God requires.

---

Footnote 8 (*cont.*)

  *The English Text with Introduction, Exposition, and Notes*, vol. 1: *Chapters 1–8*
  (NICNT; Grand Rapids: Eerdmans, 1959), p. 294.

 9. Cf. Peter H. Davids, *The Epistle of James* (NIGTC; Grand Rapids: Eerdmans,
    1982), p. 137; Martin Dibelius, *A Commentary on the Epistle of James*, revised by
    H. Greeven (Hermeneia; Philadelphia: Fortress, 1975), pp. 183–184.

## Always room for improvement

Two other texts imply that even the godliest Christians continue to battle sin in their lives. Paul is effusive in his praise of
the divine work in the Thessalonian church (cf. 1 Thess. 1:2–10;
3:1–10). They are living in a way that pleases God, and yet Paul
exhorts them to 'do so more and more' (1 Thess. 4:1). Their
significant progress in the Christian life should not be equated
with perfection. Apparently some defects remain in their lives,
so that sin continues to exist. In the same way Paul rejoices that
the Thessalonians have 'been taught by God to love one another'
(1 Thess. 4:9).[10] Indeed, they are known throughout Macedonia
for their love, and yet Paul urges them to love 'more and more'
(1 Thess. 4:10). We should not think that exhortations are directed
in the NT only to believers who are failing. Even those who are
living in love continue to need exhortations to grow in love and
godliness. One could argue that such exhortations indicate that
perfection is possible in this life and that the Thessalonians are on
the way to perfection. The other evidence we have seen, however,
suggests that even the godliest Christians have room for growth
to the end of their lives. For instance, pride continues to mani-
fest itself in subtle ways in those who have grown significantly as
believers. Those who deny the presence of any pride in themselves
are self-deceived and lacking in self-awareness.

Another text that points in the same direction is 2 Pet. 3:18:
'Grow in the grace and knowledge of our Lord and Saviour Jesus
Christ.' The call to growth indicates that the believers Peter

---

10. Paul probably refers here to the work of the Holy Spirit. So Eckhard J.
    Schnabel, 'How Paul Developed His Ethics', in Brian S. Rosner (ed.),
    *Understanding Paul's Ethics: Twentieth Century Approaches* (Grand Rapids:
    Eerdmans, 1995), p. 278. Schnabel also notes an allusion to Isa. 54:13. On
    Isa. 54:13, see Stephen E. Witmer, *'Theodidaktoi* in 1 Thessalonians 4:9: A
    Pauline Neologism', *NTS* 52 (2006), pp. 239–250.

addresses have not yet arrived. Further progress is needed in the Christian life, and hence it follows that they must still be failing and sinning, at least in some measure. Nor is it likely that Peter envisions a day in which his readers will no longer need this admonition because they have reached a plane where further growth is impossible. This epistle concentrates upon Jesus' return, maintaining that the promise of such a return should stimulate his readers to godly living (2 Pet. 3:11). It seems fair to conclude that the call to grow in grace is required until the day of that return.

## Eschatological presentation

So far, it has been argued that sin continues to bedevil believers until the day of their death, and this is true of the godliest and most devoted believers. No one is immune from sin. Such a view is confirmed by several texts which teach that believers will not be perfected until the last day, the day of eschatological presentation. Christ's work on the cross was accomplished 'so that he might present the church to himself in splendour, without spot or wrinkle or any such thing, that she might be holy and without blemish' (Eph. 5:27). The terms used here connote perfection, for the church is conceived of as a young or radiant bride without the slightest blemish or wrinkle. Holiness will become the essence of her being, so that no fault can be found in her. Such a state, however, awaits the day of eschatological presentation, when Christ returns and presents the church to the Father in all its perfection. Until that day, imperfection remains.

Colossians 1:22 is quite similar in its theme. Christ 'has now reconciled [you] in his body of flesh by his death, in order to present you holy and blameless and above reproach before him'. Believers, by virtue of Christ's death on the cross, are now friends with God; their enmity has ceased and now they belong to him. Their present reconciliation anticipates future presentation on the last day. Ultimately, believers will be perfect before God: 'holy and blameless and above reproach'. Friendship with God now does not equal perfection before God in this present evil age. The latter will be reality only on the last day.

Most of the texts that refer to an eschatological presentation also emphasize the need for growth in godliness during the present age. NT writers never consign holiness to the future with the idea that the lives of believers here and now do not matter. Believers are not and cannot be perfected now, but they are to advance in holiness until the final day. These themes are illustrated well by 1 Thess. 3:12–13: 'May the Lord make you increase and abound in love for one another and for all, as we do for you, so that he may establish your hearts blameless in holiness before our God and Father, at the coming of our Lord Jesus with all his saints.' These verses include two themes that have been the subject of our discussion. Paul prays believers will progress in their love for fellow believers and for all people. As noted previously, the call for growth seems to entail the continuing presence of sin. Believers have not yet attained the level they should. Ultimately, however, this growth in love will not be completed before the day of resurrection. Believers will be confirmed in holiness and blameless in this regard only 'at the coming of our Lord Jesus'. Final perfection will belong to believers only when Jesus returns, and hence his return is the great hope of believers, for it will be the day in which they will enjoy moral perfection (Rom. 5:2).

It seems that 1 Thess. 5:23–24 should be interpreted along the same lines as 1 Thess. 3:12–13. 'Now may the God of peace himself sanctify you completely, and may your whole spirit and soul and body be kept blameless at the coming of our Lord Jesus Christ. He who calls you is faithful; he will surely do it' (1 Thess. 5:23–24). Some in church history have understood verse 23 as support for the possibility of perfection in this life. It seems more likely, however, given the whole fabric of the scriptural witness, that the verse should be construed differently. On the one hand, Paul's prayer cannot be restricted to the last day, as if the prayer offered bears no relationship to the everyday lives of believers.

Most likely, the verse implies that believers need to continue to grow in holiness during life on earth. On the other hand, the prayer itself suggests that believers have not yet attained blamelessness, and hence continuing prayer is needed. We should not separate progress in the faith during the present age from the future consummation and completion awaited by Christians. Still, it seems that the process of growth is completed 'at the coming of the Lord Jesus Christ'. God is faithful in that he will complete the work of sanctification that has now begun in believers, and the future tense 'he will do' (*poiēsei*) points to a work of God that will be accomplished only in the future.[11] Hence there is good reason to think that perfection here is again eschatological: that it will not be the portion of believers until Jesus returns.

## Eschatological transformation

John's first epistle confirms the case being made here. The letter of 1 John is quite interesting, because on the one hand John insists that sinless perfection is impossible (1 John 1:8, 10). On the other hand, John consistently teaches that Christians are to keep God's commands (1 John 2:3–6), to love one another (1 John 2:7–11; 3:11–18; 4:7–21) and to triumph over sin (1 John 3:4–10). In the midst of this letter he writes the following: 'Beloved, we are God's children now, and what we will be has not yet appeared; but we know that when he appears we shall be like him, because we shall see him as he is. And everyone who thus hopes in him purifies himself as he is pure' (1 John 3:2–3). John marvels that believers are now God's children and exults in this present reality. He casts his gaze into the future as well, acknowledging that much is hidden from us about our future state and circumstances. Nevertheless, believers can be assured that

---

11. Rightly, C. A. Wanamaker, *The Epistles to the Thessalonians* (NIGTC; Grand Rapids: Eerdmans, 1990), p. 207.

they will be like Jesus, conformed to his image perfectly, when they see him in his glory.[12] John implicitly teaches here, therefore, that believers are imperfect now, since they will be conformed to Jesus only when they gaze upon him. At the same time, the certain hope of moral perfection motivates believers now to purify themselves and to live in a way that is pleasing to God. Even though John locates perfection to the eschaton, he does not commend moral laxity. On the contrary, the hope of being completely like Christ provokes believers to follow him even more in the present.

## Biographical examples

The continuing presence of sin in the lives of believers is also illustrated biographically. Zechariah and Elizabeth are said to be blameless in their keeping of God's commands (Luke 1:6), and yet Zechariah was struck dumb for failing to believe the words Gabriel spoke to him about the birth of his son, John (Luke 1:18–20). Zechariah's blamelessness in this context cannot be equated with sinlessness. Zechariah's unbelief reveals his sin, even though his godly life overall is quite remarkable. In the same way, a number of Peter's defects are relayed in the Gospel accounts. Some might dismiss these as occurring before Pentecost. Even after Pentecost, however, Peter sinned by acting hypocritically by refusing, because of fear, to continue to eat with Gentile believers (Gal. 2:11–14). The lapse on Peter's part scarcely suggests that his life as a whole is a failure, even though his behaviour in this instance was inexcusable. We can draw similar conclusions about Barnabas in Gal 2:11–14. Barnabas' charitable and encouraging disposition is highlighted throughout the NT. Barnabas convinced the other apostles that Paul's conversion was authentic

---

12. The consequence of seeing Jesus is that believers are made like him. So Marshall, *Epistles of John*, pp. 172–173; Smalley, *1, 2, 3 John*, pp. 146–147.

(Acts 9:27). He rejoiced over the inclusion of Gentiles into the church, and fetched Paul to assist him in ministry (Acts 11:22–26). And yet we see in Gal. 2:11–14 that he also sinned by refusing to eat with Gentile believers in Antioch. Apparently, even the godliest believers are still prone to sin and cannot claim to have reached the pinnacle of perfection in this life.

### The sinning believers at the Lord's Supper

Nor is it the case that eternal life is reserved only for those who conclude their lives on a note of triumph. The travesty taking place at the Lord's Supper in Corinth illustrates this truth (1 Cor. 11:17–34). The rich were apparently enjoying sumptuous meals while the poor were going hungry at festive meals that concluded with the Lord's Supper.[13] Indeed, some of the rich were consuming so much alcohol at these meals that they were getting drunk. No wonder Paul says that whatever was happening they were not celebrating the Lord's Supper! (1 Cor. 11:20). The Lord intervened by striking some believers with sickness and even death (1 Cor. 11:30). Such judgments, however, do not indicate that those receiving them were damned. The believers were 'disciplined so that [they] may not be condemned along with the world' (1 Cor. 11:32). In the case of those who died, the Lord cut their lives short so that they would escape final judgment. Clearly, sinlessness is not required to receive the eternal inheritance, for their behaviour at the Lord's Supper was blatantly sinful.

We must beware of using this text to cancel out the warnings

---

13. See the especially helpful essay of Otfried Hofius, 'The Lord's Supper and the Lord's Supper Tradition: Reflections on 1 Corinthians 11:23b–25', in B. F. Meyer (ed.), *One Loaf, One Cup: Ecumenical Studies of 1 Cor 11 and Other Eucharistic Texts* (Macon: Mercer University Press, 1993), pp. 75–115.

in Scripture. Those who turn against Christ and give themselves over to evil will be destroyed in the judgment. Apparently, in this instance the Lord took the lives of these believers before they committed apostasy, thereby preserving his own. This text is abused if we use it to ignore the warning passages, for the latter permeate Scripture and must be given their own voice. Furthermore, the line between sin and apostasy becomes somewhat blurred in some instances. Certainly we have a case of blatant sin here, and yet those committing it are spared by God. No one, however, should count on such an escape route when confronting the warning passages. No one can deny Jesus and think to himself, 'God will take my life and still spare me if I am going too far in my sin.' All sin is serious and, if not repudiated, leads one on a pathway that forsakes the living God. Hence we must never think that sin is trivial or inconsequential. Still, this text demonstrates that believers sin, sometimes quite dramatically. We are not always given the perspective to determine whether someone is being disciplined or has committed apostasy. Therefore, we must beware of judgments that are overly confident or presumptuous. The Lord does not give us such instructions so that we can pontificate on the future state of others. The warnings are intended for our own benefit, so that we heed them and avoid falling away. Further, they are given so that we will urgently proclaim them to others, admonishing believers to continue in the faith until the end.

### Saved through fire

Another text that is often discussed is 1 Cor. 3:10–17. Once again it is evident that believers sin and may still be saved, since some are saved 'through fire' (1 Cor. 3:15). We must be very careful with this text, however, for it is often misunderstood. In context, Paul discusses the materials used to build on the foundation, which is Christ himself. The topic arises in the midst of Paul's comments on the ministries of Apollos and himself (1 Cor. 3:5–9). Hence the

focus here is on the kind of ministry that builds on the foundation laid. The emphasis, then, is on the teaching that is erected
upon the foundation. Teaching that accords with the gospel
builds up the church, and those who teach in such a way will be
rewarded (1 Cor. 3:14).[14] Other teaching is flawed, at least to a
significant extent, and hence the work of ministry will be wasted
and will not last through the fire, though the person himself is
saved (1 Cor. 3:15). Finally, there is a kind of teaching that destroys
the church (1 Cor. 3:17). Presumably Paul has in mind here hereti-
cal teaching, and those who deviate so radically from the gospel
will themselves be destroyed and face eschatological judgment.
Occasionally I have heard teachers (I can think of a very famous
NT scholar I heard in person teach this!) say that virtually all
those who make any kind of profession of faith will be saved, no
matter how they live, but they will be saved 'through fire' if they
never show any change in their lives. Such a reading of the text is
off the mark, for notice that these very verses also have an incredibly severe warning. Those who destroy the church will themselves
face destruction. Hence, this text does not provide a warrant for
saying that one can live however he or she desires and still experience salvation. It seems in context that there is a kind of defective
teaching that does not destroy the foundation of Christ crucified.
Not every error in teaching is of the highest order. That is, even
if the teaching is defective in some respects, it is not necessarily
damning. Believers throughout church history have generally
recognized that some errors are worse than others; that some
teachings are more fundamental than others.

To sum up, 1 Cor. 3:10–17 clearly teaches that believers may
sin and still be saved on the last day. And yet this truth must be

---

14. Paul does not discuss individual believers here, but the ministries of
    church leaders: so Richard B. Hays, *First Corinthians* (IBC; Louisville: John
    Knox, 1997), pp. 55–56; Eckhard Schnabel, *Jesus and the Twelve*, vol. 1 of
    *Early Christian Mission* (Downers Grove: InterVarsity Press, 2004), p. 952.

balanced by the severe warning found in the text. A line may be crossed by which the teaching is not only defective but fundamentally destructive. As we saw in the above passage, the line between defective and destructive teaching may in some instances be difficult to draw, and any discussion of that matter would require a more detailed discussion than is possible here.

## Conclusion

In conclusion, abundant evidence exists that persevering faith cannot be equated with perfection; nor have we attempted here to include all the evidence on this matter. Believers are not perfect, for they continue to confess their sins until the day of their death. James observes in Jas. 3:2 that all believers without exception continue to sin 'in many ways'. Paul testifies that he has not been perfected (Phil. 3:12), and it is clear that perfection will not be his or ours until the day of resurrection. As long as believers have mortal bodies, they will continue to fall short of the glory of God. Even believers who are doing well spiritually need to grow in grace and knowledge (2 Pet. 3:18). There is no suggestion that believers have arrived in this life; there is always room for further growth in love (1 Thess. 3:11; 4:1, 10). Even godly believers like Zechariah, Peter and Barnabas continued to struggle with sin, and we have seen that Paul himself acknowledged that he had not yet reached perfection. The exhortations given to the churches reveal that believers were not free from sin. The writers of the NT epistles do not condemn their readers as unbelievers without further ado, even though significant sin sometimes exists in the churches. Neither, of course, do they excuse or tolerate such sin, but the point here is that they do not necessarily conclude that those in the churches are unbelievers because of their failures. Finally, a number of texts locate perfection in the eschatological presentation that will occur on the last day. Believers will be perfected only when they see Jesus at his return (1 John 3:2).

# 4. PERSEVERING IN FAITH IS NOT WORKS-RIGHTEOUSNESS

The need to persevere to the end in order to be saved sparks worries among some about works-righteousness. The gospel summons all to look to Christ for righteousness and salvation, but does the view of the warning texts proposed here shift the focus to human obedience? Does obedience play some role as the basis of justification, if one accepts the view of the warning passages suggested here? Has a Tridentine theology been smuggled in or introduced unwittingly? Has the centrality of faith been compromised, so that the Reformation emphasis on faith alone is denied? In the short scope of this chapter we can scarcely do justice to the issues raised here, but it is hoped that enough can be said in this and the next chapter to demonstrate that the view of the warning passages defended here fits with the fundamental teachings of the Reformation.

## The necessity of obedience

Is obedience necessary to obtain eternal life on the last day? The Scriptures are clear. Obedience is necessary for salvation.[1] We see this clearly in Gal. 6:8: 'For the one who sows to his own flesh will from the flesh reap corruption, but the one who sows to the Spirit will from the Spirit reap eternal life.' Sowing to the Spirit, which in the context of Galatians 6 clearly involves obedience, leads to eternal life, while sowing to the flesh results in destruction.[2] We do not need to rehearse in detail here texts such as 1 Cor. 6:9–11 that teach that those who practise evil will not inherit God's kingdom. Elsewhere Paul teaches that those who do the 'works of the flesh' 'will not inherit the kingdom of God' (Gal. 5:19–21). Paul can speak of the unsaved as those who have not 'obeyed the gospel' (Rom. 10:16). He also describes the conversion of those to whom he ministered as 'the obedience of the Gentiles' (Rom. 15:18, NASB). Indeed, the goal of Paul's mission is designed to bring about 'the obedience of faith' (Rom. 1:5; 16:26). God will judge people on the last day in accord with their works

---

1. Edwards remarks ('Persevering Faith', pp. 601–602): 'Perseverance is necessary to salvation, as 'tis a necessary prerequisite to the actual possession of eternal life. A way of persevering holiness is the way to glory, and the only way to it; and 'tis impossible that we should arrive at glory without going to it in a way of persevering holiness, as 'tis impossible that we should go from one town to another without passing the ground that is between one and the other. We read of the strait gate and the narrow way. 'Tis necessary that both should be passed, before we obtain a crown of glory. God hath set up that crown of glory at the end of a race; and therefore he that stops short of the end of the race and turns back, and so never comes to the end of the race, will never come to the crown. And so 'tis necessary for every Christian, that he should finish his course ... Perseverance in holiness is a necessary prerequisite to glory.'

2. See here Betz, *Galatians*, pp. 308–309.

(Rom. 2:6). Those who do good works will receive eternal life, but those who practise evil will face God's wrath (Rom. 2:7–10).[3] We can pose the problem even more sharply. James says that people will not be justified or saved without good works (Jas. 2:14–26). Some scholars, of course, have maintained that James does not have in mind final salvation when he says such things. But such arguments are special pleading and hardly convincing.[4] We see clearly in James that good works are necessary for justification and salvation.

Does such an emphasis on obedience cancel out *sola fide*? Not at all. The phrase 'obedience of faith' (Rom. 1:5; 16:26) is helpful here. Obedience is vital for salvation, but it is an obedience that springs from faith; that flows from faith.[5] Such a view is confirmed by 1 Thess. 1:3. Paul thanks God for the Thessalonians' 'work of faith and labour of love and steadfastness of hope'. In every instance the second noun produces the action of the first. We will look at these phrases backwards. What was it that gave the Thessalonians energy to endure and to be steadfast? Their perseverance came from their hope. So, too, the Thessalonians laboured in difficulty, but love was the spark that animated their labour. Finally, the Thessalonians are commended for their

---

3. Scholars disagree, of course, over whether the good works demanded in Rom. 2:6–10 are hypothetical. For a defence of the interpretation offered here, see Thomas R. Schreiner, 'Did Paul Believe in Justification by Works? Another Look at Romans 2', *BBR* 3 (1993), pp. 131–158.

4. Against, Earl D. Radmacher, 'First Response to "Faith According to the Apostle James" by John F. MacArthur Jr', *JETS* 33 (1990), pp. 35–41.

5. The genitive of the noun 'faith' (*pisteōs*) is likely both appositional and subjective: so Don B. Garlington, *Faith, Obedience, and Perseverance: Aspects of Paul's Letter to the Romans* (WUNT 79; Tübingen: Mohr Siebeck, 1994), pp. 10–31; John R. W. Stott, *Romans: God's Good News for the World* (Leicester: IVP; Downers Grove: IVP, 1994), p. 52.

'work'. Such work, however, sprang from faith.[6] Faith is the root and work is the fruit. Emphasizing the necessity of obedience for salvation does not threaten *sola fide* if obedience is the fruit of faith. In other words, to say that obedience is necessary for salvation is true but ambiguous. One could mean by it that works are necessary as the basis or foundation for salvation. Such a view cancels out the fundamental teaching of the gospel that our righteousness is in Christ; that we rely on the imputation of Christ's righteousness for our salvation.[7] Ultimately, our obedience is too paltry and imperfect to function as the basis for righteousness on the last day. Everything we do, as long as we are still in our mortal bodies, is still tainted by sin. Martin Luther was right in saying we are *simul justus et peccator*. We are justified and at the same time sinners. Our obedience could never function as the basis of our righteousness, because God demands perfect obedience, and only Christ obeyed perfectly. We are justified before God because we are united with Christ by faith; because we belong to the second Adam rather than the first Adam.

It is correct, however, to say that obedience is necessary for salvation as the fruit or evidence of faith. This is how I understand the teaching of James. He does not teach that works are the foundation or basis of salvation, but he does remind us that works are absolutely necessary for salvation. They are the fruit or evidence of our faith.[8] Some have told me that they do not like

---

6. Wanamaker identifies it as a subjective genitive: *Epistles to the Thessalonians*, p. 75.

7. See here the valuable work of Brian J. Vickers, *Jesus' Blood and Righteousness: Paul's Theology of Imputation* (Wheaton: Crossway, 2006).

8. Timo Laato says that faith '*only subsequently* (but nevertheless inevitably) will yield fruit': 'Justification According to James: A Comparison with Paul', *TrinJ* 18 (1997), p. 70 (italics his). Cf. also the substantive comments of Richard J. Bauckham on this matter: *James: Wisdom of James, Disciple of Jesus the Sage* (New York: Routledge, 1999), pp. 120–127.

the word 'evidence', for it suggests to them that good works are optional and unnecessary.[9] But such an understanding of evidence is not what is being defended here. Works as an evidence of faith are indispensable, not just desired or helpful, for salvation. If good works do not follow, they demonstrate that faith was not genuine. A good tree produces good fruit, and so if the fruit does not appear the tree is a bad one. One might say that if the fruit only 'shows' that the tree was bad from the beginning, whether the fruit appears is inconsequential. The only important issue is whether the tree is good or bad. But we must beware of reductionism at this very point. Whether the tree is a good or bad one is decisive, and yet it is also the case that good fruit must be present in order to obtain final salvation.

People often wonder if perfection is demanded, but we attempted to show in the last chapter that such is not the case. A new direction in life is not the same thing as perfection. The only perfect righteousness is the righteousness of Christ. The NT writers do not offer us percentages so as to delineate exactly how much change is needed to show that faith is genuine. Attempting to calculate how much obedience is needed misses the point of the demand for obedience in the NT witness. Any such approach would encourage a rabbinical or mishnaic type of discussion that is foreign to the spirit of the NT.

We have also shown in the last chapter that perfection is not demanded, but that the very best believers fall short in many ways. In this chapter we see that what God calls for fundamentally is faith: trust in him. Believers run the race to the end (Phil. 3:12–16) not by concentrating on doing good works, but by faith. Running the race to the end means that we look to Christ for

---

9. Cf. here the words of Edwards ('Persevering Faith', p. 603): 'Those promises of eternal life to perseverance are for the comfort of the saints; for the more a person by experience finds that his goodness is of a persevering kind, the more evidence has he of his title to life.'

righteousness, instead of ourselves. What it means to persevere, then, is not to gauge how far we have come but to keep clinging to Christ until the end. The good fruit comes not as we look to ourselves but as we deny any self-righteousness and find our righteousness in Christ. The call to perseverance, in other words, is a call to faith, not a call to work up the energy to make it to the end by our own strength.

## The cross in Galatians

Paul reproaches the Galatians because they began their new life in faith and tried to complete it by works (Gal. 3:1–5). He clarifies that, just as one begins the new life by the power of the Spirit and by faith in Christ, so too one continues the Christian life in the same way. We do not begin in the Spirit and try to be perfected in the flesh. Hence the Christian life from start to finish is a call to trust God. Every step of the way, we look to Christ for our righteousness. Those who stumble and fall may be restored again and again, as long as they keep running the race by looking to Christ for salvation and putting their trust entirely in him.

The paradox here is quite striking. If we concentrate on the quality of our works, we are apt to become consumed with ourselves and our righteousness. The pathway is thereby opened to pride and self-delusion. We may fail to see how dramatically we fall short of what God requires. The call to persevere, however, should be understood in a radically different way. We are summoned to look to Christ rather than ourselves; to put our hope in Christ's death and resurrection; to remind ourselves daily that our only hope at the day of resurrection is in what Christ has done for us. The good works that follow, then, are the fruit of looking to Christ, trusting in Christ alone and clinging to the cross alone for our righteousness.

Such an interpretation is borne out in the NT. We noted earlier the severe warning in Galatians if the Galatians adopt circumcision in order to be saved (Gal. 5:2–6). If they do so, they will be separated from Christ and face damnation. Paul's warning, however, is scarcely a call for believers to look to themselves for righteousness. It is precisely the opposite. If the Galatians received circumcision, they were trusting in what they could accomplish for eschatological salvation. Paul summons them, on the contrary, to look to the cross alone for their righteousness. The call to persevere is nothing other than a call to look outside of themselves to Christ for every good gift.

The interpretation we propose is confirmed by the centrality of the theme of the cross in Galatians.[10] In this letter Paul sets up a radical polarity between circumcision and the cross. Those who trust in obeying the law and in circumcision repudiate the cross of Christ. Seeing the pervasiveness of the cross in Galatians is quite instructive. Jesus 'gave himself for our sins to deliver us from the present evil age' (Gal. 1:4).[11] Those who revert to circumcision for righteousness are falling back into the present evil age, instead of relying upon the deliverance Christ accomplished at the cross. Galatians 2:15–21 probably functions as the thesis statement of the letter.[12] Paul concludes by saying: 'I do not nullify the grace of God, for if righteousness were through law, then Christ died for no purpose.' Those who attempt to obtain righteousness by keeping the law make Christ's death superfluous. If forgiveness may be obtained by the law and the Sinai covenant, then circumcision is required and there is no need for Christ's death on the cross. Paul argues, however, that keeping the law cannot bring salvation, and hence Christ's death is the only hope of believers.

---

10. Rightly, Robert A. Bryant, *The Risen Crucified Christ in Galatians* (SBLDS 185; Atlanta: Society of Biblical Literature, 2001), pp. 163–194.

11. For the importance of eschatology, or what Martyn calls apocalyptic, see J. Louis Martyn, 'Apocalyptic Antinomies in Paul's Letter to the Galatians', *NTS* 31 (1985), pp. 410–424.

12. Betz identifies it as the *propositio* of the letter: *Galatians*, pp. 18, 114.

Paul is utterly mystified, therefore, when he considers the attraction the Galatians have to circumcision. He exclaims: 'O foolish Galatians! Who has bewitched you? It was before your eyes that Jesus Christ was publicly portrayed as crucified' (Gal. 3:1). It is as if someone has cast a spell on the Galatians, because they no longer see the significance of Christ's death. The Galatians claim to believe in Jesus' death, but if they receive circumcision to be right with God they fundamentally deny the atoning significance of the crucifixion.

Returning to the law would lead to a curse rather than a blessing, for the law demands perfect obedience (Gal. 3:10), and no one can attain such a standard. The curse can only be removed through Christ's death. 'Christ redeemed us from the curse of the law by becoming a curse for us – for it is written, "Cursed is everyone who is hanged on a tree"' (Gal. 3:13). If the Galatians reverted to the law-covenant and circumcision, they would stand under a curse because of their disobedience to the law. The only way to escape the curse and to receive the blessing of being part of Abraham's family is by putting one's trust in Christ's substitutionary work on the cross, by which he took upon himself the curse that humans deserved.[13] Perseverance, then, consists in continuing to trust in the cross of Christ. Apostasy, in this instance, focuses on trusting human ability to keep the law and turning away from Christ and him crucified.

The same theme emerges in Galatians 4. To live under the law is to be enslaved to the elements of the world (Gal. 4:1–3). The Sinai covenant and the law belong to the old era of salvation-history (Gal. 4:1–7; cf. Gal. 3:15–25). A new era has now dawned. 'But when the fullness of time had come, God sent forth his Son, born of woman, born under the law, to redeem those who were under the law, so that we might receive adoption as sons' (Gal. 4:4–5).

---

13. See especially, here, Timothy George, *Galatians* (NAC; Nashville: Broadman & Holman, 1994), pp. 240–242.

The new age has been inaugurated by the cross of Christ, by which he has freed those who were under the dominion of sin and the law. Devotion to circumcision and the law leads to bondage instead of freedom. Apostasy, in Galatians, means that one leaves the freedom won by Christ for the bondage of keeping the law.

The radical disjunction between circumcision and the cross is emphasized in Gal. 5:11: 'But if I, brothers, still preach circumcision, why am I still being persecuted? In that case the offence of the cross has been removed.' Circumcision in and of itself is insignificant to Paul (Gal. 5:6; 6:15; 1 Cor. 7:19). If circumcision is required for right-standing with God and eschatological salvation, it stands in fundamental opposition to the cross, for the cross focuses on the utter spiritual poverty of human beings and locates our righteousness in Christ alone. The cross is an offence because it proclaims the weakness, the ungodliness and the inability of human beings to please God. It calls upon us to place all our hope for righteousness in Christ, and such a message is a great scandal for all who worship themselves and are entranced with their ability. Perseverance, then, is nothing other than grasping the scandal of the cross until the day we die. The same theme is enunciated in Gal. 6:12–13. 'It is those who want to make a good showing in the flesh who would force you to be circumcised, and only in order that they may not be persecuted for the cross of Christ. For even those who are circumcised do not themselves keep the law, but they desire to have you circumcised that they may boast in your flesh.' The false teachers promote circumcision because it panders to human pride and exalts human ability. A message that lauds human potential and righteousness is so very attractive, but it undercuts the cross, which reminds us daily that we 'are wretched, pitiable, poor, blind, and naked' (Rev. 3:17). Perseverance does not mean that we are self-satisfied with our righteousness. It means that we are conscious of our misery every day, and continue to turn to Christ for the cleansing of our sins.

Given the emphasis upon the cross in Galatians, we are not surprised that the letter closes with the affirmation: 'But far be it from me to boast except in the cross of our Lord Jesus Christ, by which the world has been crucified to me, and I to the world' (Gal. 6:14). Human beings boast either in the cross or in their own righteousness: in what God has done for them or what they have done for God. Paul closes the letter with the statement 'From now on let no one cause me trouble, for I bear on my body the marks of Jesus' (Gal. 6:17). The marks made by circumcision benefit no one. The only scars that matter are those that come because one trusts in Christ's cross.

Martin Luther rightly said about justification on the basis of keeping the law, 'Trying to be justified by the Law is like counting money out of an empty purse, eating and drinking from an empty dish and cup, looking for strength and riches where there is nothing but weakness and poverty, laying a burden on someone who is already oppressed to the point of collapse, trying to spend a hundred gold pieces and not having even a pittance.'[14]

Our brief survey on the cross in Galatians assists us in understanding the warning passage in Gal. 5:2–4 that was examined previously in this book. Those who turn to circumcision for salvation and attempt to be justified by the law gain no benefit from Christ's sacrifice because they have repudiated it as the way to be right with God. In Galatians, therefore, apostasy means that one reverts to trusting in oneself for salvation. It is clear, then, that perseverance is not perfection. It means that one looks to Christ and the cross for forgiveness; that one stakes everything on the righteousness that comes from Christ; that one is deeply conscious of one's sins and realizes that only Christ can provide forgiveness. Faith, according to Galatians, then finds its object in Christ and his cross and resurrection. Paul does not teach that one can begin in the Spirit and be perfected in the flesh (Gal. 3:3). Faith looks away from human ability and performance to Christ.

---

14. Martin Luther, *Lectures on Galatians, 1535*, vol. 26 of *Luther's Works*, edited by Jarislov Pelikan (St Louis, MO: Concordia, 1963), pp. 406–407.

Faith recognizes the rebellion and sickness of our hearts and looks only to Christ for the forgiveness of sin.

## The cross in Hebrews

The warning passages in Hebrews, as noted previously, are probably the severest in the NT. Significantly, they have much the same import as the warning in Gal. 5:2–4. It is likely that Jewish Christians who were tempted to relapse to a form of Judaism are primarily addressed in Hebrews.[15] Throughout the letter the author argues for Christ's superiority over the law. Christ is superior to the angels who were the mediators of the Mosaic law (Heb. 1:1 – 2:18), and he is superior to Moses who transmitted the law to the people (Heb. 3:1 – 4:13). His Melchizedekian priesthood makes obsolete the Levitical priesthood and the Mosaic law (Heb. 4:14 – 10:18).[16] Reverting to the Sinai covenant and the Levitical priesthood is criticized with a battery of arguments. The Levitical priesthood was fundamentally ineffective because it never brought perfection or genuine forgiveness of sins. Jesus' priesthood is of a different order, since he is not from the tribe of Levi (Heb. 7:13–14). His priesthood is in accord with the order of Melchizedek (Ps. 110:4). The Melchizedekian priesthood takes precedence over the Levitical one, for Levi in a sense paid tithes to Melchizedek, showing that Levi was inferior to Melchizedek (Heb. 7:4–10). Further, the Melchizedekian

---

15. D. A. Carson and Douglas J. Moo, *An Introduction to the New Testament*, 2nd edn (Grand Rapids: Zondervan; Leicester: Apollos, 2005), pp. 609–612. Against, W. G. Kümmel, who identifies the recipients as Gentile Christians: *Introduction to the New Testament*, rev. edn, trans. by Howard Clark Kee (Nashville: Abingdon, 1975), pp. 398–400.

16. On Jesus as the high priest in Hebrews, see Mathias Rissi, *Die Theologie des Hebräerbriefs: Ihre Verankerung in der Situation des Verfassers und seiner Leser* (WUNT 41; Tübingen: Mohr Siebeck, 1987), pp. 55–70.

priesthood is eternal, while the Levitical priesthood is provisional (Heb. 7:11–12, 17, 23–25), and since Jesus functions as a priest for ever, the salvation won by him is irrevocable. The Melchizedekian priesthood was instituted with an oath, whereas the Levitical priesthood lacked one, and hence the covenant of the former supersedes the latter (Heb. 7:20–22). Christ's sacrifice is definitive and final, for Levitical priests offered sacrifices on earth, but Christ's sacrifice brings us into the very presence of God in heaven (Heb. 9:23–24). Further, his sacrifice did not need to be repeated, but was effective once-for-all (Heb. 9:25–26). The repetition of animal sacrifices demonstrates that such offerings did not truly and permanently atone for sins (Heb. 10:1–3). If they secured atonement, they would not need to be offered on a regular basis. Indeed, unwilling animals can scarcely provide forgiveness of sins (Heb. 10:4–10). Only Christ's sacrifice is sufficient, for he is a willing and human sacrifice. Indeed, Jesus Christ is not only fully human but also fully divine (Heb. 1:1–14), and hence his priesthood brings assurance of final and total forgiveness. The Levitical priests continue to stand offering sacrifices, but Christ sits because his work is finished, and forgiveness has been secured once-for-all (Heb. 10:11–14). The forgiveness of sins promised in the new covenant (Jer. 31:31–34) has truly been accomplished in the cross of Jesus Christ (Heb. 10:18).

The brief summary of the significance of Christ's sacrifice in Hebrews provides immense help in comprehending the warning passages. Occasionally the author has been understood as a rigorist whose message does not fit with the gracious gospel found in Paul. In actuality the warning passages accord with what Paul argued in Gal. 5:2–4. The author of Hebrews argues that if the readers turn to Levitical sacrifices and the Sinai law, then there is no hope of salvation for them. They cannot repudiate Christ's sacrifice and hope to obtain eternal life on the last day. The author does not commend perfection to his readers. Rather, he exhorts them to continue to hold onto Jesus Christ; to continue to cling to his sacrifice for forgiveness of sins. They are tempted to turn away from Christ and to rely on the law for eschatological salvation. In so doing they would be turning away from the gracious provision of the gospel (final forgiveness of sins) and would revert to a priesthood that does not offer final forgiveness. They would rely on sacrifices that always pointed to the sacrifice of Christ. But if one rejects what the OT sacrifices pointed to in salvation-history, then the 'pointers' themselves cannot secure forgiveness. If one rejects the fulfilment of the type (Jesus' sacrifice), then the types themselves (animal sacrifices) cannot avail.

The author of Hebrews, then, does not call his readers to works-righteousness or to perfection. He summons them to keep trusting in Christ as the only basis for the forgiveness of their sins. Believers can 'draw near . . . in full assurance of faith' because they have been 'sprinkled clean from an evil conscience and . . . washed with pure water' (Heb. 10:22).[17] Assurance comes, then, not from looking to themselves but from focusing on what Christ has accomplished for them at the cross. Faith does not become fixed on good works, but on Christ and his cross. 'There no longer remains a sacrifice for sins' if the Hebrews fall away (Heb. 10:26), because no one can be forgiven for sins who rejects the final and definitive sacrifice for sins.

Apostasy in Hebrews, then, as in Galatians, occurs when believers cease clinging to Christ and his atonement. Believers persevere by continuing to find their forgiveness and final sanctification in Christ instead of themselves. Hebrews does not call upon believers to look to themselves, but to Christ. Those who commit apostasy end up looking to themselves and trusting in themselves. Assurance is found only by those who lean upon the sacrifice of Christ.

The view proposed here is confirmed by the great faith chapter

---

17. Many scholars see a reference to baptism here: see Attridge, *Hebrews*,
    p. 289; William L. Lane, *Hebrews 1–8* (WBC; Dallas: Word, 1991), p. 287;
    F. F. Bruce, *The Epistle to the Hebrews* (NICNT; Grand Rapids: Eerdmans,
    1964), pp. 250–251.

in Hebrews 11. It is not my intention to do a thorough study of its teaching on faith. What is of interest is the light the chapter casts on the issues that concern this book. The OT persons mentioned are all commended for their faith. Indeed some of the names mentioned might raise eyebrows, because in the OT their sins play a prominent role in the narrative. For instance, Samson's life fell short of God's will in many respects (Judges 13–16), and yet he is commended for his faith (Heb. 11:32). In the same way, Gideon, Barak and Jephthah (Heb. 11:32), though they trusted the Lord in some remarkable ways, also displeased the Lord because of their lack of faith and the sins they committed. One could argue that the author of Hebrews glosses over their sins and selects famous persons from the OT without considering carefully what they did. A good case can be made, however, for the view that the author knew the OT stories well and did not distort the OT. Samson functions as a good case study. How could the author of Hebrews commend him for his faith when he sinned so blatantly with Delilah and failed on quite a few other occasions? A careful reading of the narrative in Judges indicates that the interpretation of Samson's life in Hebrews is not far-fetched. The remarkable feats performed by Samson were undertaken only with the strength given to him by the Lord. Even after his sin with Delilah, when Samson was in prison, the Lord had not forsaken him. The narrator informs us that his hair began to grow again in prison (Judg. 16:22). This observation about Samson's hair is highly significant, for it indicates that the Lord had not forsaken him. Furthermore, the narrator in Judges clearly believed that Samson died gloriously (Judg. 16:28–30). He avenged himself on the Philistines and brought about a great slaughter at his death. Indeed, he called upon the Lord to strengthen him so that the pillars upon which the house rested would give way when he pushed upon them. Obviously, the narrator of the story believed that Samson's prayer was answered. Further, we can see why the author of Hebrews perceived faith in Samson's prayer, for he looked to the Lord to answer his petition.

The inclusion of Samson in the heroes of faith supports one of the main themes in this book. Samson, despite all his flaws and foibles, did not commit apostasy. Perseverance to the end in Hebrews does not mean perfection! The example of Samson is remarkably helpful, since some have read Hebrews as if it were incredibly rigorous. Hebrews warns readers to keep clinging to Christ to the end. Remarkable failures may occur along the way, but they are not the same thing as apostasy if one repents and turns to Christ anew. We can see, therefore, why the author of Hebrews includes others, such as Barak, Gideon and Jephthah. In his view genuine faith cannot be equated with perfection. Those who please God are those who continue to trust him, even though their lives continue to be tainted by sin.

Nor is it convincing to limit what is argued for here to minor characters in Hebrews 11. Abraham and Moses receive significant attention in Hebrews 11 as men of faith, and yet it is apparent from reading the OT that they sinned in a number of ways. Abraham lied about Sarah being his wife on two occasions (Gen. 12:10–20; 20:1–18) and failed to trust God by resorting to Hagar to have an heir (Genesis 16). Moses sinned by killing the Egyptian (Exod. 2:11–12); by not trusting the Lord to give him strength to lead the people out of Egypt (Exod. 4:10–16); and by striking the rock when God told him to speak to it (Num. 20:8–12). And others mentioned fit the picture sketched in here: Noah got drunk (Heb. 11:7; Gen. 9:21); Jacob's faults are evident in the narrative (Heb. 11:21; Gen. 25–35); and David committed adultery with Bathsheba and murdered Uriah (Heb. 11:32; 2 Samuel 11). None of these men are indicted in Hebrews because of their sins. Instead, they are featured for their faith. Indeed, no OT believer, in Hebrews or anywhere else in the NT, is ever criticized for the sins they committed. The failure to note their sins cannot be chalked up to the ignorance or faulty reading of NT authors. The sins of OT believers were not unknown. Indeed, the sins of Abraham and David are alluded to in Rom. 4:1–8. Still, what we see in Hebrews 11 and the rest of the NT is quite instructive. The silence of the

NT regarding the sins of OT believers compels us to take notice. The NT and Hebrews 11 bear witness that OT believers lived in a way that is pleasing to God. God does not remember their sins, but their trust in him. When Samson is remembered, he is recalled not as a failure but as a hero of faith. Human beings tend to focus on shortcomings, but the Lord testifies to their trust in him.

Hebrews 11, then, confirms that the life of faith is not a life of perfection. Indeed, it is evident that many of the believers commended were deeply flawed, just as we are today. The significance of this observation increases when we realize that Hebrews contains the strongest warnings in the NT. The writer warns against falling away from Jesus; he does not teach perfection. Believers are to be like Samson, who, despite his sins, continued to put his trust in the Lord and presumably repented of his sin. The life of perseverance is a life of faith and repentance. It places all its trust in what Jesus as the great high priest accomplished on the cross. It looks away from self and looks to Christ.

## The denials of Peter and Thomas Cranmer

We must also consider here the story of Peter's denials. We must not remove the strength of Jesus' words, that Jesus will deny the one who denies him (Matt. 10:32–33). What is quite startling is to find that Peter denied Jesus three times (Matt. 26:69–75). The gravity of such a denial must be acknowledged, for such a blatant denial calls into question whether Peter belonged to Jesus. Still, there are differences between Peter's denial and Judas's betrayal. Judas planned his betrayal in advance and conspired to hand Jesus over to the religious leaders (Matt. 26:14–16). Peter, on the other hand, on the very night he denied Jesus, was quite confident that he had the stamina and fortitude to die with Jesus (Matt. 26:33–35). Peter's denial, then, was not premeditated. He gave in to a sudden overwhelming fear when temptation struck. Naturally, there is still no excuse for Peter's sin, but we have a hint that Peter's denial is not of the same import as Judas's betrayal. Yes, Peter denied Jesus, but he later repented of his denial. He faced the humiliation of admitting his wrongdoing and did not hide in the darkness of his evil (John 3:19–21). He repudiated his denial and came to Jesus for cleansing and forgiveness. Hence Jesus' words that the one who denies him will be denied on the last day refers to an *ultimate* denial. Peter's repentance demonstrated that his denial was short-lived. His return to Jesus indicated that he was running the race in faith again, trusting in Jesus' righteousness for his vindication before God on the last day.

The story of Peter could easily be abused and exploited for wrong ends. No one should rationalize that they too will deny Jesus and then repent later. Such a mindset reveals a mind dramatically different from Peter's before his repudiation of the Christ, for Peter was supremely confident that he would never deny Jesus and apparently believed that he was ready to die with him (Matt. 26:35). Jesus' severe warning must not be trifled with in such a fashion. On the other hand, a harsh and unyielding view of the warnings must also be avoided. The story of Thomas Cranmer is remarkably similar in some ways to the denial of Peter.[18] When Queen Mary assumed the throne in 1553, Cranmer was stripped of his power and imprisoned. He was threatened with death unless he recanted of his teachings. Fear gripped Cranmer as he contemplated the prospect of being burned at the stake, and so he recanted what he taught. But Cranmer's recantation was not the last word. The Holy Spirit began to work on his heart as he was in prison. He regretted signing the recantation. The authorities had decided to make an example of him, requiring him to read his recantation before his death. But Cranmer surprised those in power when he boldly recanted his recantation, expressing great

---

18. See *Foxe's Christian Martyrs of the World from the Celebrated Work* by John Foxe, new revised and illustrated (Chicago: Moody Press, n.d.), pp. 493–508.

regret for his denial of the gospel. He pledged to put his right hand that signed the recantation in the fire first, to signal his sorrow for and repentance of his sin. And when he was burned at the stake, many witnesses saw Cranmer put his right hand that had signed the recantation in the fire first to show his repentance and regret for his sin. Once again, the issue is ultimate and final and definitive denial of Jesus. Neither Peter nor Cranmer finally denied Jesus. They failed in the race, but they repented and began running again. Perseverance should never be equated with perfection. What it means to persevere is to keep trusting Jesus until the end. Those who persevere have the same experience as the man with the demonized son. They cry out, 'I believe; help my unbelief!' (Mark 9:24). Those who persevere are deeply conscious of the continued unbelief in them, but they keep clinging to Jesus and trusting in him for forgiveness of sins until the last day. Both Peter and Cranmer were deeply aware of how short they had fallen, but they were not destroyed by their failures because they did not trust in themselves but in the one who saved them.

## Concluding thoughts

I am not denying that a living faith leads to a transformed life. Some could read the last two chapters and underestimate the transforming power of God's grace. We must be careful not to overestimate or underestimate the change that occurs in our lives. Hebrews 11, after all, tells us that 'by faith Abraham . . . obeyed' (Heb. 11:8). Genuine trust in God means that there are changes in the lives of those who know God. Abraham staked his entire future on God's promise (Heb. 11:8–16). He left his homeland, friends and family because of his faith in the promise of God. He was filled with assurance that God would fulfil his promise of offspring through Isaac, so that he was willing to offer him up in sacrifice, knowing that God would raise him from the dead if he was slain (Heb. 11:17–19). Moses was so convinced that God's promises were true that he abandoned a life of luxury in Egypt and identified with the people of God, suffering with them while waiting for the final reward (Heb. 11:23–26). Perseverance cannot be equated with perfection, but neither is it a cipher. Those who trust in Christ, according to the NT witness, live a transformed life.

The NT emphasizes constantly that those who know God keep his word. The evidence that one truly knows God is the keeping of his commandments (1 John 2:3–6; 3:4–10). Clearly, John is not teaching perfectionism here, but a new way of life does accompany faith in Christ. There is a new direction, a new obedience, imperfect as it is. One indication that one is a believer is that one loves fellow believers (1 John 2:7–11; 3:11–18; 4:7–21). Those who are born of God, according to John, practise righteousness (1 John 2:29), keep God's commandments (1 John 3:9) and love fellow believers (1 John 4:7). Faith is living and active and it leads to obedience.

The dynamic character of faith is clearly taught in James's famous text on justification by works (Jas. 2:14–26). It is not my purpose here to engage in a full exegesis of these verses. I would argue that the works necessary for justification and salvation are evidence of a true and living faith. Saving faith embraces Christ as the crucified and living Lord. Dead faith exists only in the intellect and assents to doctrines about Christ and salvation, but does not truly rest in Christ. Saving faith, however, looks to Christ alone for salvation and trusts in him entirely. Hence all good works stem from faith, and thus James does not contradict the teaching that salvation is by faith alone. He simply reminds us that genuine faith always produces works.

# 5. FAITH AND ASSURANCE AND WARNINGS

## Assurance

This book concludes with a return to the warning passages. If the warnings are addressed to believers and threaten eternal punishment, how can believers have assurance that they will escape final judgment? Does not such a view of the warnings lead to the conclusion that some of those who truly belong to God may forsake their salvation and be lost for ever? Such a view of the warnings fits with Arminian theology, and it certainly deserves respect as a possible reading of the NT. Many Christians I know come close to dismissing such a teaching as heresy, but such a judgment is rash and fails to see, in my opinion, that the Arminian reading of the warnings is not far-fetched. One of the advantages of such an interpretation is that the warnings are taken seriously, and hence believers are rightly warned about the consequences of falling away from Christ. I

fear that some other viewpoints may grant to some who are per-
ishing a false assurance, with idle words about the security of the
believer. Still, I will argue here that the view that genuine believers may lose their salvation is unpersuasive.

The problem with the Arminian reading is that those adher-
ing to it do not have a persuasive reading of assurance texts in
Scripture, whereas the Reformed view has a more convincing
explanation of the warning texts. For instance, Paul assures the
Philippians that 'he who began a good work in you will bring it
to completion at the day of Jesus Christ' (Phil. 1:6). Arminians
read this text to say that the good work will be completed,
provided that one continues to believe and if one does not fall
away. Such a reading, however, drains the verse of virtually all
comfort. All believers who know the sinfulness of their own
hearts fear that they will not have the strength to make it to the
end. Furthermore, the text indicates that God initiated the good
work of faith in believers and promises that he will complete what
he has started. Nothing is said here about some kind of coopera-
tive effort that may ultimately fail because of one's lack of faith.
Moreover, if God does not give faith, then precisely how did he
begin the good work in the lives of believers? We seem to be left
with a situation in which God externally encouraged faith but did
nothing to produce it internally. But the text points to a divine
work in believers which will reach its promised consummation on
the last day.

The same line of argument applies to Rom. 8:35–39, where Paul
promises that nothing will separate believers from the love of
Christ. Again, the Arminian argues that nothing external can separate believers from Christ's love, but believers may be detached
from Christ by their own choices.[1] Such a reading of the text is
unconvincing. Paul clarifies that nothing 'in all creation' can sever

---

1. Cf. Wesley, *Explanatory Notes Upon the New Testament*, p. 551; Marshall, *Kept by the Power of God*, p. 103.

believers from Christ's love (Rom. 8:39), and the human will is certainly part of created reality.[2] Hence what humans will choose is included implicitly by Paul. Further, the kinds of things that would cause someone to choose apostasy are listed. Why would someone forsake Christ? We can imagine that believers might deny him if they faced 'tribulation, or distress, or persecution, or famine, or nakedness, or danger, or sword' (Rom. 8:35). The very point Paul makes here is that even the most terrifying experiences will not move one to forsake Christ. The reason for the believer's faithfulness does not lie in the strength of the believer's will but in the love of Christ, which keeps them even through agonizing sufferings. The love of Christ is so compelling that believers are protected and kept by God, so that they are never separated from his love.

We see the same truth in John's Gospel.[3] Jesus taught that all those given by the Father to the Son will come to Jesus (John 6:37), whereas no one can come to Jesus unless he or she is drawn by the Father (John 6:44). If all those given by the Father to the Son come to Jesus and put their faith in him (John 6:37), and only those drawn by the Father are able to come, then it follows that the grace of God is an effective grace. It secures a believing response in those given by the Father to the Son. These verses are parallel to Phil. 1:6 when it speaks of the good work that God began in believers. John 6, however, does not conclude with initial belief. Jesus promises several times in this text as well that he will raise on the last day those given by the Father to the Son (John

---

2. See especially here, Judith M. Gundry Volf, *Paul and Perseverance: Staying in and Falling Away* (Louisville: Westminster/John Knox, 1990), pp. 57–58; Moo, *Romans 1–8*, p. 589.

3. For a very helpful exposition of the tension between divine sovereignty and human responsibility in John's Gospel, see D. A. Carson, *Divine Sovereignty and Human Responsibility: Biblical Perspectives in Tension* (Atlanta: John Knox, 1981).

6:39, 40, 44, 54). Here the resurrection pledged belongs only to believers, and Jesus promises that all those given by the Father to the Son will attain the resurrection of life. In other words, the good work begun will surely be completed by the resurrection. Hence the promise of the resurrection corresponds to the second part of Phil. 1:6, where Paul speaks of God completing the good work that he has begun. In John the resurrection denotes that work of accomplishment.

John 10:28–29 runs along the same lines as John 6. 'I give them eternal life, and they will never perish, and no one will snatch them out of my hand. My Father, who has given them to me, is greater than all, and no one is able to snatch them out of the Father's hand.' Eternal life is by definition irrevocable, for those who receive it 'will never perish'. Both the Father and the Son protect believers, so that they will always remain within the flock of God. Arminians, of course, argue that even though no outsider can remove someone from God's protection, one's own free will can do so. Reading the text conditionally violates the most natural interpretation, for Jesus promises that those who receive eternal life 'will never perish'. The implication is that such life is inviolable, and that no created reality, even free will, can overcome the power of the life given. The promise gives comfort because God's grace is so effective that those who have eternal life never forsake the one who has saved them.

### Federal Vision

Another interpretation has been proposed by some within the Calvinist tradition. Some are proposing what is labelled as the Federal Vision.[4] They argue that no one who is elect can lose their

---

4. It is not my purpose here to discuss the Federal Vision in any detail, for that would take us too far from the present project. Naturally, there

salvation, in contrast to the Arminian view. But they also argue that one may be a member of the new covenant and not be part of the elect. Hence the warnings in the NT are addressed to covenant members, and some covenant members are not truly saved. Some in the church of Jesus Christ, therefore, truly apostatize and fall away from the faith. Hence one may be a member of the new covenant while not being truly elect. The benefit of this view is that the warnings are genuine: they threaten final judgment, and some actually commit apostasy. Still, the Federal Vision must be distinguished from Arminianism, for those who commit apostasy are not the elect but those who, though participants in the new covenant, were not also chosen by God to be saved.

This view of the new covenant is quite fascinating, but also fails to persuade. It is quite clear from the OT texts that the new covenant promised forgiveness of sins and the gift of the Holy Spirit (Jer. 31:31–34; Ezek. 11:18–20; 36:26–27).[5] Indeed, Hebrews emphasizes that forgiveness of sins has been accomplished once-for-all through the atoning death of Christ (Heb. 10:11–18). The same OT background is reflected in the Lord's Supper tradition, where Jesus' blood is understood covenantally, with the result that it brings forgiveness of sins (Matt. 26:28). In 2 Corinthians 3 the distinctiveness of the new covenant is located in the gift of the Spirit, so that the law is written on the heart, in contrast to the external character of the Sinai covenant.

Distinguishing between the elect and the members of the new covenant is quite unconvincing. The NT emphasizes that the gift of the Spirit is the *sine qua non* for belonging to the people of God. Paul assures the Galatians that circumcision is unnecessary

---

are differences of emphasis with the Federal Vision movement, which cannot be examined here.

5. I think it is warranted to include the texts from Ezekiel under the new covenant, even though that terminology is not used by Ezekiel. Ezek. 37:26 speaks of 'a covenant of peace' and 'an everlasting covenant'.

to belong to the family of Abraham (Gal. 3:1–5). The proof that they belong to Abraham is the gift of the Spirit that they enjoy. So too, during the Jerusalem Council a debate over terms of entrance into the church of Jesus Christ took place (Acts 15:1–29). Some argued that Gentiles were required to be circumcised and to observe the law of Moses to be saved. Peter retorted that observance of the law was a yoke that could not be borne (Acts 15:7–11). Indeed, the gift of the Spirit demonstrated that Gentiles were truly members of God's people. Further, Paul's argument in Romans 8 links together those who are chosen by God and those who have received the Spirit. Those who have the gift of the Spirit as a down payment are assured of obtaining the final inheritance (Eph. 1:13–14). Those who have the Holy Spirit belong to God (Rom. 8:9). This new wrinkle among a few Calvinists is rather strange, for now some who enjoy the gift of the Holy Spirit and are forgiven for their sins may lose their salvation, while the elect will never be forsaken. I would argue that the exegetical warrant for dividing the recipients of the Spirit from the elect is unwarranted. The Arminian view, that all true believers may lose their salvation, is more consistent than a view that drives a wedge between the elect and those who have the Holy Spirit and enjoy forgiveness of sins.[6]

---

6. Naturally, a much fuller discussion is needed of the issues raised here. For a helpful discussion representing both those for and against the Federal Vision, see E. Calvin Beisner (ed.), *The Auburn Ave Theology, Pros and Cons: Debating the Federal Vision* (Fort Lauderdale, FL: Knox Theological Seminary, 2004). E. Calvin Beisner in the conclusion of the book puts his finger on some of the inconsistencies regarding the nature of the covenant in the Federal Vision and some of the problems raised for the assurance of believers ('Concluding Comments on the Federal Vision', pp. 305–325). For a critique of the Federal Vision, see Guy Prentiss Waters, *The Federal Vision and Covenant Theology: A Comparative Analysis* (Phillipsburg, NJ: Presbyterian & Reformed, 2006).

## The warnings as means

Instead of adopting the Arminian view or the Federal Vision reading, I will argue for still another perspective. The warnings are addressed to believers and threaten them with eternal destruction if they fall away. I would contend that all true believers (all the elect, all those who have the Holy Spirit and enjoy the forgiveness of sins and are members of the new covenant) heed the warnings and are thereby saved. In other words, the warnings are one of the means God uses to keep his own trusting him and persevering in faith until the end.[7] Such perseverance must not be equated with perfection. It is nothing other than clinging to the cross of Christ for the forgiveness of sins until the last day. To say that the warnings are a means by which believers are preserved does not teach that one's perseverance is the basis of righteousness at the last judgment. Those who persevere are those who are conscious of the fact that they are blind, miserable, poor and naked until the last day. They look to the righteousness of Christ for their salvation, not to their own perseverance. And yet they do persevere in trusting Christ. They do not abandon him finally and definitively. The warnings provoke them to continue to look to Christ and his righteousness.

What is distinctive is the claim that all believers heed the warnings and are thereby saved. It is crucial to remember here that the warnings are *prospective*, admonishing the readers about what will happen if they fall away. We can easily slip into the habit of reading the warnings as *declarations*, as if they announce the condemnation of those who have fallen away. The latter approach interprets the warnings *retrospectively* rather than *prospectively*. To do so, however, wrests the warnings from the function they play in the NT letters.

---

7. Edwards remarks ('Persevering Faith', p. 608): 'Though it be promised that true saints shall be so influenced and assisted, as that they shall persevere; yet this is one means by which God influences them, viz. counsels and warnings against falling away.'

Typically the warnings have an if–then character, saying that *if* one falls away *then* destruction will follow. Conditional clauses with an if–then structure should not be construed as already fulfilled conditions. To read 'if you drink poison, you will die' as a fulfilled condition misreads the conditional sentence.[8] The condition constitutes a warning, and the contingency must be fulfilled for the consequence to follow. The reason the warning is given, of course, is so that the contingency will not be fulfilled. We give urgent warnings not to drink poison so that no one will do so.

The warnings in the NT, then, do not rebuke readers for falling away. They urge them most earnestly not to do so. They are signposts along the way, calling upon believers to keep trusting Christ in spite of the many difficulties in their lives. They summon readers to keep drinking from Christ as the fountain of living waters (John 4:14). They are like letters from a trusted counsellor to a married couple contemplating divorce, where the counsellor urges the couple most strenuously that divorce would have fatal consequences. They are words along the way, admonitions in the

---

8. Fanning reads the conditional statements in Heb. 3:6 and 3:14 to say that the Hebrews are already members of the people of God and saved if they endure to the end ('A Classical Reformed View', pp. 206–218). He suggests that the conditions here do not designate a cause–effect relationship but an evidence-to-inference relationship. Space is lacking to interact with Fanning in detail here. Even if one agrees that some conditions should be construed as evidence to inference, it is more natural to read the conditions in Heb. 3:6 and 3:14 as presenting a contingent situation in which the apodosis is fulfilled if the protasis is fulfilled. Fanning turns the conditions in Heb. 3:6 and 3:14 into retrospective reflections. The major problem with Fanning's view is that the other conditional statements in Hebrews are prospective, and thus it is quite unlikely that the conditions in Heb. 3:6 and 3:14 would function differently from the other conditions in the letter. Rightly, Osborne, 'A Classical Arminian View', p. 231; Cockerill, 'A Wesleyan Arminian View', pp. 242–244.

flow of life, designed to prevent readers from making a decision that will lead to their ruin. We saw this quite clearly in Galatians and Hebrews. The readers must not turn to the law for their righteousness, but must rely solely and utterly on Christ's death and resurrection for them.

The main objection that is raised against this reading of the warnings is that the warning is drained of all significance if it cannot be fulfilled. If the elect always and inevitably fulfil the warning, then what is the point of giving the admonition? To return to an illustration used earlier: if no one will ever drink poison, it is quite superfluous to have a warning on poison bottles. The problem with this objection is that it assumes that the warning plays no role or function in keeping believers from falling away. The warnings are read from an abstract global perspective and are deemed as inconsequential since no true believer can fall away. But what is argued here is that the warnings are means God uses so that believers do not fall away. The other day I was reversing and almost hit a parked car behind me, but my son cried out, 'Dad, stop!' His warning caused me to put on the brakes and prevented me from hitting the car. In the same way, it is because, when my children were small, I threatened punishments if they ran into the street, they never ran into the street. Warnings are not abstractions. They are the means God uses to keep believers from falling away.

## Acts 27

It is important to note, first of all, that admonitions are given even when God promises that what is warned will not occur. We see this vividly in Acts 27. When Paul sailed to Rome, a horrendous storm imperilled the lives of Paul and everyone on the ship. In the midst of the storm Paul received a revelation from God, a promise that the life of everyone would be spared. Paul shared this revelation with all those on board (Acts 27:21–25):

Since they had been without food for a long time, Paul stood up among them and said, 'Men, you should have listened to me and not have set sail from Crete and incurred this injury and loss. Yet now I urge you to take heart, for there will be no loss of life among you, but only of the ship. For this very night there stood before me an angel of the God to whom I belong and whom I worship, and he said, "Do not be afraid, Paul; you must stand before Caesar. And behold, God has granted you all those who sail with you." So take heart, men, for I have faith in God that it will be exactly as I have been told.'

God promised, then, that every single person would survive physically: that not a single life would be lost.

One could easily conclude that such a promise would rule out any need for a warning. If I had been Paul, I might have gone down into the hold of the ship and started a party, knowing that no matter what I did, every single person's life would be spared. Paul, however, conducted himself quite differently. As the sailors drew near to land they took soundings, for they had craftily planned to leave the ship in the dinghy. Acts recounts the story as follows (27:30–32):

And as the sailors were seeking to escape from the ship, and had lowered the ship's boat into the sea under pretence of laying out anchors from the bow, Paul said to the centurion and the soldiers, 'Unless these men stay in the ship, you cannot be saved.' Then the soldiers cut away the ropes of the ship's boat and let it go.

The presence of the warning here is quite remarkable. Paul warned that if the sailors were allowed to leave the ship, then the people on board would not survive. Their lives would be lost without the sailors to guide the ship. Apparently Paul did not think that the promise of life for all excluded the need for a warning. Indeed, Paul's warning functioned as one of the means by which the lives of all those on board were spared. Further, the warning was effective for *every single person*. The threat was that the people in the ship would not live if the sailors escaped in the dinghy. The warning is not robbed of significance, even though the threat held before them did not come to pass. It was certainly true that they would not have lived if the sailors had snuck away in the dinghy.

The application to the question before us is clear. It does not logically follow that the warning lacks force if the threat does not come to pass. By definition, the threat comes to pass only if the condition is fulfilled. If every person warned avoids fulfilling the condition, then the threat is averted. If such a state of affairs occurs (everyone avoids fulfilling the condition), it does not follow that the warning was meaningless. But this is precisely what is being argued for here. The warnings to the elect are not meaningless simply because the threat never comes to pass for those who are truly saved. The elect escape the threatened judgment precisely by heeding the warning. And I would contend that *all* the elect heed the warning, and hence they never will face final judgment. Such a state of affairs does not mean that the warning was superfluous or unnecessary. That is akin to saying that warning my children not to run into the street was clearly unnecessary since none of them ever got run over. I could reply, 'But they did not get run over because I warned them not to run into the street.'

Recently, it has come to my attention that Herman Bavinck argued the same position regarding the warnings in Scripture. Bavinck remarks:

> Now the question with respect to this doctrine of perseverance is not whether those who have obtained a true saving faith could not, if left to themselves, lose it again by their own fault and sins: nor whether sometimes all the activity, boldness, and comfort of faith, actually ceases, and faith itself goes into hiding under the cares of life and the delights of the world. The question is whether God upholds, continues, and completes the work of grace he has begun, or whether he sometimes permits it to be totally ruined by the power of sin. Perseverance . . . is a gift of God . . . He watches over it and sees to it that the work of grace is continued and completed. He

does not, however, do this apart from believers but through them.
In regeneration and faith, he grants a grace that as such bears an
inadmissible character; he grants a life that is by nature eternal; he
bestows the benefits of calling, justification, and glorification that are
mutually and unbreakably interconnected. All of the above-mentioned
admonitions and threats that Scripture addresses to believers,
therefore, do not prove a thing against the doctrine of perseverance.
They are rather the way in which God himself confirms his promise
and gift through believers. They are the means by which perseverance
in life is realized. After all, perseverance is also not coercive but, as
a gift of God, impacts humans in a spiritual manner. It is precisely
God's will, by admonition and warning, morally to lead believers to
heavenly blessedness and by the grace of the Holy Spirit to prompt
them willingly to persevere in faith and love. It is therefore completely
mistaken to reason from the admonitions of Holy Scripture to the
possibility of a total loss of grace. This conclusion is illegitimate as
when, in the case of Christ, people infer from his temptation that
he was able to sin. The certainty of the outcome does not render the
means superfluous but is inseparably connected with them in the
decree of God. Paul knew with certainty that in the case of shipwreck
no one would lose one's life, yet he declares, 'Unless these men stay in
the ship, you cannot be saved.' (Acts 27:22, 31)[9]


## 2 Thessalonians 3:3 and Matthew 6:13

One could also object that the example adduced from Acts 27
relates to physical life, not spiritual salvation. Such an objection
is not compelling, for the *principle* of how warnings function
applies to both spheres. In addition, other texts point to the same

---

9. Herman Bavinck, *Reformed Dogmatics*, vol. 4, *Holy Spirit, Church and New Creation*, edited by John Bolt, translated by John Vriend (Grand Rapids: Baker, 2008), pp. 267–268.

principle in the spiritual sphere. For instance, Paul assures the Thessalonians, 'But the Lord is faithful. He will establish and guard you against the evil one' (2 Thess. 3:3). When Paul speaks of the Lord's faithfulness, he often assures believers that God will keep them from apostasy and preserve them to the end (cf. 1 Cor. 1:9; 10:13; 1 Thess. 5:24; 2 Tim. 2:13). Here too God's faithfulness is such that he will preserve believers from the devil and strengthen them so that they never fall away. Here we have a *promise* of final spiritual preservation. What is striking in 2 Thess. 3:3 is the allusion to the final petition in the Lord's Prayer, 'And lead us not into temptation, but deliver us from evil' (Matt. 6:13). Probably Jesus here has in mind deliverance from the evil one, and hence the connection to 2 Thess. 3:3 is quite likely.

What is instructive is comparing these two texts. On the one hand, 2 Thess. 3:3 *promises* that God will protect his own from the evil one. On the other hand, Matt. 6:13 *petitions* the Lord to 'deliver us from evil'. We face the same tension observed in Acts 27. What need is there to ask the Lord to deliver us from evil if he has already promised to do so? If a father promises to take his son to a basketball game, the son does not need to ask the father to do so, unless he fears that the father is unreliable, forgetful, or unfaithful. Such an illustration, however, fails to grasp the character of the biblical witness and views God's promises as abstractions. Both the promise and the petition must be included to get a full-orbed picture of reality. We cannot play off the promise against the petition so that the need for the petition is eliminated. Nor can we play off the petition against the promise so that the promise is falsified. God promises he will protect every believer from the evil one, and there are no exceptions to this stunning promise. On the other hand, believers are to pray to the Lord that he will deliver them from the evil one. One of the means God uses to deliver believers from the evil one is their prayer. And given the nature of the promise, we have good reason to believe that the petition to be spared from the devil's attack is always answered in the affirmative. One might object that the petition in the Lord's Prayer is not always answered affirmatively, since believers still sin, but this objection does not succeed against what is being argued for here. I am not claiming that believers never sin. Instead, I understand the petition to ask that believers would never commit apostasy.[10] These two texts, then, illustrate well the thesis defended here. We have a condition: believers must pray to be delivered from the evil one. We also have a promise: God will protect believers from the evil one. The promise for final protection from the devil will certainly be answered in the lives of all the elect, but such a promise does not mean believers do not need to pray the last petition in the Lord's Prayer. This petition is one of the means God uses to fulfil the promise. The promise and the petition are not enemies but friends.

## Mark 13

Another example of the same phenomenon appears in the eschatological discourse in Mark 13. Jesus affirms that 'the one who endures to the end will be saved' (Mark 13:13). Unparalleled sufferings and tribulations are in store for disciples (Mark 13:19). Indeed, if the Lord had not abbreviated the days of such suffering, no one would be saved (Mark 13:20). 'But for the sake of the elect, whom he chose, he shortened the days' (Mark 13:20). The salvation in view here is likely not physical preservation but eschatological salvation. In other words, if the suffering were more intense, the elect would apostatize because of the ferocity of the persecution. The Lord, however, so controls events that he protects the elect from apostasy. The suffering does not become so intense that they deny the Lord.

The subsequent verses confirm the idea that apostasy is at stake here. Disciples are warned to be on guard against putting their

---

10. For this view, see the previous discussion on Matt. 6:12 in Chapter 3, under 'Prayers for forgiveness'.

faith in false christs (Mark 13:21–22). Surely the heart of apostasy consists in believing in a false christ! An error on this matter is no minor quibble, for those who do not believe in Jesus as the Christ will face eternal judgment. Further, the signs and wonders of the false christs and prophets will dazzle and confound many, so that they will believe in what is false. Jesus remarks that the miracles will be so extraordinary that they would 'lead astray, if possible, the elect' (Mark 13:22). What must be seen here is that it is not possible for the elect to be led astray. The signs and wonders would sway the elect if such were possible, but such a state of affairs is impossible. The Lord has cut short the days so that the elect will be saved; so that they will not be deceived. In other words, all of the elect, despite the terror and deception of such days, will remain faithful to the Lord. Not one of them will fall away or be deceived. We have an implicit promise here. All the elect will continue to believe that Jesus is the Christ, despite the intense tribulation which they will endure.

Still, the promise of final salvation does not rule out the mandate that the disciples themselves must endure to be saved (Mark 13:14). They must 'be on guard' (*blepete*), lest they believe in false christs (Mark 13:23). Mark again repeats that they must 'be on guard' (*blepete*) and 'keep awake' (*agrypneite*) in such evil days (Mark 13:33). The importance of vigilance is underlined again with the parable for servants (Mark 13:34–36). The door-keeper must 'stay awake' (*grēgorē*) while the owner of the house is gone (Mark 13:34). By all means the servants must 'stay awake' (*grēgoreite*), so that they will be ready for the master's arrival (Mark 13:35). And the chapter concludes once again with the same warning, 'And what I say to you I say to all: stay awake' (*grēgoreite*, Mark 13:37). The urgent and repeated warnings to watch, to stay vigilant and to keep awake are striking. Believers must remain vigilant to receive an eternal reward. They must be alert, so that they do not fall prey to false christs. Only those who persevere to the final day will be saved.

What is the purpose of such urgent warnings to endure and

to watch, if it is not possible for the elect to fall away? We saw above that the Lord has shortened the days so that the elect will certainly be saved. The chosen are promised that it is impossible for them to fall away. The reception of such a promise does not cancel out, however, the need for the warning. Those who have a sure promise of final salvation are also warned most urgently to be vigilant and to stay awake, so that they will obtain final salvation. The promise of salvation should lead not to lassitude but to vigilance and endurance. Heeding the warnings is one of the means by which the promise of final salvation is obtained on the last day. All those who are elect will certainly respond to the call to vigilance and be saved, but it does not follow from this that the warnings are inconsequential for believers.

John Calvin came to very similar conclusions on Mark 13:21–22, explaining that the promise is sure, even though believers are exhorted to be on their guard.

> This was added for the purpose of exciting alarm, that believers may be more careful to be on their guard; for when such unbounded freedom of action is allowed to *false prophets*, and when they are permitted to exert such powers of deceiving, those who are careless and inattentive would easily be entangled by their snares. Christ therefore exhorts and arouses his disciples to keep watch, and at the same time reminds them that there is no reason for being troubled at the strangeness of the sight, if they see many persons on every hand led away into error. While he excites them to solicitude, that Satan may not overtake them in a state of sloth, he gives them abundant ground of confidence on which they may calmly rely, when he promises that they will be safe under the defense and protection of God against all the snares of Satan. And thus, however frail and slippery the condition of the godly may be, yet here is a firm footing on which they may stand; for it is not possible for them to fall away from salvation, to whom the Son of God is a faithful guardian. For they have not sufficient energy to resist the attacks of Satan, unless in consequence of their being *the sheep of Christ, which none can pluck out of his hand* (John x. 28). It must therefore

be observed, that the permanency of our salvation does not depend on us, but on the secret election of God; for though our salvation is *kept through faith*, as Peter tells us (1 Pet. i. 5), yet we ought to ascend higher, and assure ourselves that we are in safety, because the Father hath given us to the Son, and the Son himself declares, that *none who have been given to him shall perish* (John xvii. 12).[11]

## Perseverance as a means and the initial call of the gospel

Perhaps some still believe that the warnings cannot play a significant role if believers will certainly persevere. How one interprets such a state of affairs also depends upon other theological commitments, which are based on the interpretation of many other texts that cannot be investigated here. Such an objection certainly makes sense from an Arminian perspective, for in their view the warnings lead to the conclusion that believers may lose their salvation. I argued briefly that such a reading, though understandable, does not do justice to the texts that promise eschatological salvation to believers, for God pledges to complete the good work he has started. Hence warnings and assurance are not enemies but friends. By heeding the warnings believers gain assurance in their lives.

It should also be pointed out that a Reformed reading of the warnings fits with a Calvinist interpretation of how believers are saved in the first place. God elects who will be saved before the foundation of the world (Eph. 1:4–5). He chooses who will be saved in his own good pleasure, not on the basis of human choices or even faith (Rom. 9:10–23). Faith is a gift God grants to some and not to others, and hence believers cannot even boast about

11. John Calvin, *Commentary on a Harmony of the Evangelists, Matthew, Mark, and Luke*, trans. by William Pringle (reprint; Grand Rapids: Baker, 2005), 3:141 (italics his).

exercising faith (Eph. 2:8–9). My intention here is not to defend such a reading in detail, for such has been done elsewhere.[12] What must be noted here, however, is that God's election of some does not invalidate the call to believe. When the gospel is proclaimed, those who preach do not summon the hearers to consider whether they are elect or chosen by God. Rather, they consistently call upon their auditors to repent and believe (e.g. Acts 2:38; 3:19; 16:31). One could object that the summons to believe is completely unnecessary, for God has promised to save only the elect. Arminians in particular object that if the elect will certainly believe, then the call to belief is superfluous. But the Calvinist responds that the preaching of the gospel is the means God uses to bring his own to faith. On a Calvinist scheme, the need to believe in order to be saved is not minimized in the least even though God has chosen who will believe from the foundation of the world. Belief is a *condition* to be saved, but God through his grace has promised to fulfil that condition in the lives of his elect. Still, such a promise does not eliminate the urgency of believing when the gospel is proclaimed. Those who hear must believe and repent to be saved, and they are summoned to respond with the utmost urgency.

What is being argued here is that the warning passages should be understood along the same lines as the initial call of the gospel. God has promised that his elect will persevere, just as he promised to grant faith to his chosen ones. Such a promise does not eliminate the need to persevere. Both the summons to persevere and the initial call to believe in the gospel are conditions that must be fulfilled to be saved, but in both instances God grants the grace so that the conditions will certainly be fulfilled in those who belong to him. The certainty that God will grant perseverance

12. See for instance Thomas R. Schreiner and Bruce A. Ware (eds), *Still Sovereign: Contemporary Perspectives on Election, Foreknowledge, and Grace* (Grand Rapids: Baker, 2000).

does not remove the moral urgency to persevere in faith, just as the certainty that God will grant faith to the elect does not lessen the need to believe. Some Calvinists think the warning passages are superfluous if believers will certainly heed the warnings, but this no more follows than saying that preaching the gospel is superfluous if the elect will certainly be saved. In both instances, the call to believe and the call to persevere are means God uses to bring about the final salvation of his own.

When we say that the call to persevere is a means of salvation or a condition of salvation, are we falling prey to works-righteousness? It is only works-righteousness if our perseverance in faith is the ground of our salvation. Faith is a condition for salvation and a means of salvation, but it cannot be construed as the *basis* of salvation but the *instrument* of salvation. Faith unites a believer to Christ as Saviour and Lord. So too, heeding the warnings is not the basis of salvation. We have seen throughout this book that believers continue to be tainted with sin throughout their lives, until the day of redemption. Warnings are one of the means God uses, however, to save his people. But this is scarcely works-righteousness, for the warnings call upon believers to continue to trust in Christ and his righteousness for their salvation. We saw in both Galatians and Hebrews that it was the false gospel based on works that was tantalizing the Galatians and the Hebrews. Paul and the author of the Hebrews called upon their readers to keep trusting Christ for their salvation. Believers are warned against beginning in the Spirit and trying to be perfected in the flesh. Those who heed the warnings are simply continuing to trust Christ and his righteousness instead of relying on the flesh and one's own works. The warning passages, then, are nothing other than a call to continue to believe. It is not as if believers begin by trusting Christ and then the warnings summon them to trust in themselves and their good works. The warnings call believers away from themselves and admonish them to continue to believe in Christ to receive the eschatological reward.

## What about those who fall away?

I have argued thus far that the warnings in the NT are directed to believers, and they threaten final judgment. At the same time, all those who belong to God and are called by his grace will heed the warnings. The God who first called them to faith will strengthen them so that they do not fall away. God's promise to keep them does not rule out the significance of human responsibility. Believers are summoned to persevere and to continue in faith to the end. The dynamic at work here is similar to the initial call to faith. On the one hand, God elects his own and grants them grace, and hence faith is a gift of God. On the other hand, human beings are called upon to believe and trust in the gospel. God's gracious election does not cancel out the need for human beings to believe in order to be saved. Nor does the responsibility to believe lead to the conclusion that divine election is a charade. The warning passages, I have maintained, function in the same way as the initial call to faith. God promises to preserve his own until the end. Such a promise, however, does not mean that perseverance is optional (just as faith is not optional to obtain salvation).

Now, if the view argued for in this book is correct, how do we account for those who fall away, especially since I have argued that the elect do not fall away? It is precisely here that we must keep in mind the *function* of the warnings. They are *prospective*, admonishing believers to keep clinging to Jesus Christ, so that they do not turn to idols (1 John 5:21). The warnings were not written as *retrospective* reflections on the status of those who had already fallen away. They are instructions shouted to runners during a race, so that they will not give into exhaustion and discontinue running. They are instructions given to troops in the midst of the battle. They are not armchair reflections on those who deserted during the battle. Given the function of the warnings, we are not surprised that some of the questions we typically pose to these texts are not answered by the warning texts themselves.

Nevertheless, some texts in the NT speak of those who have fallen away; of those who did not persevere to the end. The first letter of John is written to grant assurance to those who did not fall away, so that they will know they have eternal life (1 John 5:13). John exhorts them to remain faithful to the original teaching they have received. The exhortation is given because some have left the church and presumably formed a new community. The deviant teaching in this instance does not come from outside the church; it hails from those who were once members of the church but have now left the community. How does John evaluate those who have left the church who were formerly members? Have they lost their salvation? The answer is clearly given in 1 John 2:19: 'They went out from us, but they were not of us; for if they had been of us, they would have continued with us. But they went out, that it might become plain that they all are not of us.' Those who fall away were never truly Christians. They 'were not of us'.[13] Perseverance is the mark of genuineness, and those who do not persevere reveal that they were not genuinely part of the people of God. Here is the retrospective view that is missing from the warnings.[14] No one who is truly elect will ever fall away, for those who do apostatize reveal that they were never genuinely saved.

Nor is such a view limited to 1 John. Jesus speaks of remarkable works that would seem to be possible only for Christians, and yet he clarifies that some who do such works will not receive eternal

---

13. Dale Moody misreads this text to say they 'went out from us because they were no longer of us': *The Word of Truth: A Summary of Christian Doctrine Based on Biblical Revelation* (Grand Rapids: Eerdmans, 1981), 357. Such an interpretation is hardly persuasive, for the word 'no longer' (*ouketi*) is not found in the text. What John says is that 'they were not (*ouk*) of us'. No indication is given that John considered those who left the community to be formerly genuine believers.

14. To say they are missing from the warnings is no criticism of the warning passages. We must not expect every text to answer all of our questions.

life. 'Not everyone who says to me, "Lord, Lord," will enter the kingdom of heaven, but the one who does the will of my Father who is in heaven. On that day many will say to me, "Lord, Lord, did we not prophesy in your name, and cast out demons in your name, and do many mighty works in your name?" And then will I declare to them, "I never knew you; depart from me, you workers of lawlessness"' (Matt. 7:21–23). Prophesying in Jesus' name, exorcising demons and doing spectacular miracles is no guarantee of eternal life. Indeed, 'many' will do such works and be consigned to perdition. Nonetheless, they confess Jesus as 'Lord, Lord.' Hence we might conclude that they, as genuine members of the church, had forsaken a salvation they once enjoyed. But the text actually does not permit such a view. Jesus says, 'I never knew you.' The text does not say 'I once knew you but now repudiate you.' Rather, they were never genuinely part of the people of God. They appeared to be believers but were not genuinely so. Only those who are poor in spirit (Matt. 5:3) and do God's will (Matt. 7:21) are genuine believers.

Two other examples illustrating those who have wandered from the faith will be provided from Pauline writings. In Ephesus, Hymenaeus and Philetus introduced deviant teaching, claiming that the resurrection had already occurred (2 Tim. 2:18). As a result they were 'upsetting the faith of some' (2 Tim. 2:18). The term 'upsetting' (*anatrepō*) denotes the overturning of the faith of some in the church. The same verb is used when Jesus 'overturned [the] tables' of the money-changers (John 2:15). Some departed from the faith under the influence of Hymenaeus and Philetus. At first glance it seems that they committed apostasy. But Paul immediately adds these words: 'But God's firm foundation stands, bearing this seal: "The Lord knows those who are his," and, "Let everyone who names the name of the Lord depart from iniquity"' (2 Tim. 2:19). To say that the foundation of God's house stands means that those who are truly part of God's household never depart from it. This seems to be confirmed by the citation from Num. 16:5, which affirms that the Lord knows those who are truly his.[15] Paul alludes here to the apostasy of Korah, Dathan and Abiram. Their rebellion demonstrated that they did not truly belong to the Lord. So too, those who are truly part of God's house will not be swayed by deviant teaching. The foundation of the house remains unshakable. Apostasy occurs, then, among those who are in the church, but those who fall away reveal that they never truly belonged to God – that they were not part of God's house. Hence the apostasy is phenomenological. In other words, those who appeared to be true believers (but actually were not) fall away, but no true believer falls away.

Another text along the same lines appears in 1 Cor. 11:19. Paul remarks that 'there must be factions among you in order that those who are genuine among you may be recognized.' Paul rebukes the Corinthians in this context for their selfish conduct during the Lord's Supper (1 Cor. 11:17–34), for the rich are eating sumptuously and some are even getting drunk, while the poor do not have enough to eat. Paul is astonished that such behaviour is occurring at meals that culminated with a celebration of the Lord's death. The divisions, however, have at least one benefit, according to verse 19. They show who is 'genuine' among the Corinthians. The term 'genuine' (*dokimos*) denotes those who are truly Christians (cf. 2 Cor. 10:18; 13:7; 2 Tim. 2:15).[16] The word

15. Rightly, Mounce, *Pastoral Epistles*, pp. 528–529. Against, Marshall, who restricts the reference to the church (*Pastoral Epistles*, pp. 755–756). A reference to the church is included, provided that a distinction is made between those who are elect and those who fall away and prove thereby they were not elect and were never genuine believers. So George W. Knight III, *The Pastoral Epistles* (NIGTC; Grand Rapids: Eerdmans, 1992), pp. 415–416.

16. The divisions in the church will reveal who truly belongs to Christ (so Fee, *First Corinthians*, pp. 538–539; Hays, *First Corinthians*, p. 195; Anthony C. Thiselton, *The First Epistle to the Corinthians* (NIGTC; Grand Rapids: Eerdmans, 2000), pp. 858–859). Against, David E. Garland, who thinks

'unapproved' (*adokimos*) in Paul regularly denotes unbelievers
(Rom. 1:28; 1 Cor. 9:27; 2 Cor. 13:5, 6, 7; 2 Tim. 3:8; Titus 1:16; cf.
also Heb. 6:8). The divisions among the Corinthians reveal, then,
the genuine believers in the congregation. In other words, some
of those who claimed faith were not truly believers. Again, Paul
does not argue that anyone has lost the salvation they already had.
The divisions within the congregation bring to the surface who is
a genuine believer and who does not truly belong to God.

When we think of the warnings in the NT, as I have argued
throughout this book, we see that they are addressed to believers,
and that they are *prospective* instead of *retrospective*. The NT authors
do not couch the warnings so that they are limited to those who
only appear to be believers or to false believers. The warnings
are explicitly directed to believers, and responding to such warnings is no trivial matter. Believers obtain eschatological salvation
by continuing to believe until the end and by heeding the warnings given to them. Nor do NT authors warn their readers in
order to dampen their assurance or to cause them to question
whether they belong to God. The admonitions are not intended
to provoke introspection, so that readers doubt whether they are
truly saved. As Cockerill says, 'these warnings were not given to
generate worry about whether one had apostatized'.[17] Rather, the
warnings are given so that the readers will continue to believe. In
other words, the warnings do not quench assurance but are one
of the means the Lord uses to strengthen it.[18] When parents warn

---

Footnote 16 (*cont.*)
   the approved refer to the elite members of the community sociologi-
   cally: *1 Corinthians* (BECNT; Grand Rapids: Baker, 2003), pp. 538–539.
17. 'A Wesleyan Arminian View', p. 291.
18. Robert N. Wilkin fails to understand this and hence he argues that
   Caneday and I teach that believers cannot have assurance of salvation
   before death: 'Striving for the Prize of Eternal Salvation: A Review
   of Schreiner and Caneday's *The Race Set Before Us*', *Journal of the Grace*

a child, 'Don't run into the street,' the child is not supposed to ask himself, 'I wonder if I am alive.' The warning is intended to preserve the child's life, not to raise questions about whether the child is truly alive. Too often interpreters subvert the warnings, reading them as if they are asking whether one really believed in the past. Many Christians, in my experience, read these passages in such a way and mistakenly fall into deep introspection over whether they are genuinely Christians. Jonathan Edwards has wise words in this regard:

> It is not God's design that men should obtain assurance in any other way than by mortifying corruption, and increasing in grace, and obtaining the lively exercises of it. And although self-examination be a duty of great use and importance, and by no means to be neglected, yet it is not the principal means by which the saints do get satisfaction of their good estate. Assurance is not to be obtained so much by *self-examination* as by *action*. The Apostle Paul sought assurance chiefly this way, even by 'forgetting the things that were behind, and reaching forth unto those things that were before, pressing towards the mark for the prize of the high calling of God in Christ Jesus; if by any means he might attain unto the resurrection of the dead.' And it was by this means chiefly that he obtained assurance: I Cor. ix. 26, 'I therefore so run, not as uncertainly.' He obtained assurance of winning the prize, more by running than by considering. The swiftness of his pace did more towards his assurance of a conquest than the strictness of his examination.[19]

There is a place for such introspection, as Edwards indicates (2 Cor. 13:5). My point is that the warning texts themselves call

---

*Evangelical Society* (Spring 2002), p. 7. Actually, we argue precisely the opposite.

19. Jonathan Edwards, *The Religious Affections* (reprint; Carlisle, PA: Banner of Truth, 1986), p. 123.

not for introspection but for action. They are not written so that believers will ask whether they are Christians, but so that believers will keep living as Christians.

Even though the warnings are specifically addressed to believers, surely the authors knew that some of those warned did not truly belong to God. It would be highly artificial for authors to write: 'Beloved, I write to you who are not authentic Christians.' And if the warnings were couched in this way, true believers would think that they were off the hook – that the warnings were not addressed to them. I have argued, however, that God uses the warnings to motivate believers to persevere, so that the warnings play a vital role in believers obtaining eternal life on the last day. Hence it makes eminent sense that the warnings are addressed to believers, because such admonitions are one of the means God uses to motivate believers to cling to Christ and his righteousness for salvation. The warnings call upon believers to continue to exercise faith until the last day. We cannot say that the warnings are superfluous simply because believers always heed them.

On the other hand, some failed to heed the warnings.[20] We have seen that those who fell away never knew God; that they revealed by their failure to persevere that they did not truly belong to Christ's flock. The warning passages themselves do not address themselves to the question of the state of those who are addressed. Indeed, such reflection would be quite strange in a warning, since its intent is to prevent believers from falling away, not to consider the final status of the readers before they respond to the warning. Nor do the NT writers intend to split readers into two groups before the warnings: first, those who are truly saved, and second, false believers. Such an approach would

---

20. It must be said again that the function of the warning passages themselves is not to answer the question posed here. We derive what is said here from retrospective texts; and the warning passages function prospectively.

render the warnings highly artificial. The NT authors, after all, did not know in advance who in the churches were inauthentic. They were not given infallible knowledge about the spiritual state of their readers. The writers also exercised a judgment of charity in writing to their congregations, assuming that the readers were genuine believers. They did not view their readers suspiciously, doubting that a genuine work of grace had occurred in them. They are confident that the warnings given will produce a positive result and will provoke believers to keep trusting in Christ. We noted earlier the severe warnings in Gal. 5:2–6 and Heb. 6:4–8. But Paul is full of confidence in Gal. 5:10 that the Galatians will respond to his admonition and will not fall away.[21] He knows that those who have begun in the Spirit (Gal. 3:3) will not end up finally yielding to the flesh, and that the one who began the good work in them will complete it (Phil. 1:6). 'I have confidence in the Lord that you will take no other view than mine, and the one who is troubling you will bear the penalty, whoever he is' (Gal. 5:10). In the same way, the author of Hebrews is confident that his readers will respond to his warnings and be saved. 'Though we speak in this way, yet in your case, beloved, we feel sure of better things – things that belong to salvation' (Heb. 6:9).

The writers, of course, addressed churches as a whole. They were convinced that a genuine work of grace had occurred. This is not to say, however, that every single individual in the churches was truly saved. Certainly some fell away, and in some instances the authors must have been surprised at those who defected.[22] In such instances the retrospective vision of the NT applies: they were never truly part of Christ's flock. Is such a view contradicted

---

21. Cf. here, Bruce, *Galatians*, p. 235; J. Louis Martyn, *Galatians: A New Translation with Introduction and Commentary* (AB; New York: Doubleday, 1997), p. 475; J. D. G. Dunn, *The Epistle to the Galatians* (BNTC; Peabody: Hendrickson, 1993), p. 277.

22. Perhaps Paul was surprised at Demas' defection (2 Tim. 4:10).

by Heb. 6:4–6? I have argued that those addressed are specifically addressed as Christians. Furthermore, the argument of this book is that the warnings are the means the Lord used to keep them on the right and good way. But is the writer insisting that every last one of his readers was a believer? Again, it must be noted that the author does not reflect on whether there are false believers in their midst. The author believes that the warnings are part and parcel of the gospel; that all believers (including himself!) need exhortations to continue in the faith until the final day. Warnings are one of the means God uses to keep believers running in the race, so that they keep trusting in Christ. Still, it does not follow from this that the author of Hebrews is claiming that every person who received the letter was truly a believer. The function of the warning is to address believers. And the argument of this book is that all true believers heeded the warning. Is it possible that some addressed departed from the faith? Certainly. And if one were to ask the writer of Hebrews this question: what if some do not heed your warnings – are they truly believers? I think he would have said, 'They are Esaus in the midst of Jacobs (cf. Heb. 12:15–17). They were never truly part of God's people. But all those who are truly believers need the warnings, and they will heed God's admonitions as well, for God's grace will secure the desired response.'

# EPILOGUE

I have argued in this book that the warnings and admonitions in the Scriptures have a particular function. By them believers are warned against departing from Christ and the gospel. If they do apostatize, then they will face final damnation. In other words, the idea that the warnings relate only to the losing of rewards which are beyond eternal life is mistaken. The admonitions and threats in the Scriptures address the issue of life eternal. Nor are the warnings addressed to those who are nearly Christians. They are addressed to those who have received the Holy Spirit; to those who are genuine Christians.

If the warnings are directed to Christians, do they quench and dampen our assurance? Certainly not. The admonitions are the means God uses to keep believers on the path of faith. Believers are even more assured of their salvation as they heed the warnings, because their response to the warnings demonstrates that they truly belong to God. And the argument of this book is that the elect and those in the new covenant *always heed the warnings*. God loses none of those who belong to him. Just as all the elect believe the gospel when it is proclaimed to them, so too all those who are foreknown and predestined will certainly be glorified. God's promise that all those who are his will persevere does not exclude the need to heed the warnings. As we have seen, heeding the warnings is the means by which believers are preserved on the last day.

Nor should such perseverance until the end be confused with perfection or with works-righteousness. As believers, we fall into sin daily and regularly call out for the forgiveness of our sins. Believers do not advertise their own righteousness in enduring to the end. Instead, they cling to Christ and his righteousness until the day of redemption. They look away from themselves and what they have accomplished and put their hope in Christ crucified and risen. Those who persevere are not perfect, but they never turn away from Jesus Christ. They never forsake him as the fountain of living waters. They do not put their trust in their own works, but in the atonement secured by Jesus Christ. Perseverance, then, does not lead to pride but to humility, for it is nothing other than clinging to Christ and his righteousness. We show our trust by obeying, for there is no other way to receive the prize on the last day.

# SERMON:
# WARNING! LIVE BY FAITH ALONE
# (GALATIANS 5:2–12)

Paul teaches us in Galatians that we are righteous by faith alone. We are so prone as believers to trust in our feelings instead of in the gospel. But we are not righteous by our feelings. Martin Luther remarks that we can be full of anxiety and fear in the corners of our hearts. Despair can grip us as we begin to think of ourselves. I quote:

> As sinners we say to ourselves, 'I feel the violent terrors of the Law, and the tyranny of sin, not only waging war against me but completely conquering me. I do not feel any comfort or righteousness. Therefore, I am not righteous but a sinner. And if I am a sinner, then I am sentenced to eternal death.'

But Luther gives us ammunition to battle against such a view. He says:

But battle against that feeling, and say, 'Even though I feel myself completely crushed and swallowed by sin and see God as a hostile and wrathful judge, yet in fact this is not true; it is only my feeling that thinks so. The Word of God, which I ought to follow in these anxieties rather than my own consciousness, teaches much differently, namely, that "God is near to the brokenhearted, and saves the crushed in spirit" (Ps. 34:18), and that "He does not despise a broken and contrite heart" (Ps. 51:17).'

Let's come to our text this morning. First, we see in Galatians 5:2–4 that trust in our works will lead us to hell: 'Look: I, Paul, say to you that if you accept circumcision, Christ will be of no advantage to you. I testify again to every man who accepts circumcision that he is obligated to keep the whole law. You are severed from Christ, you who would be justified by the law; you have fallen away from grace.'

Verse 2 begins with a solemn introduction. Paul reminds the readers of the seriousness of the situation by reminding them that he speaks with authority and absolute seriousness. If they accept circumcision *for salvation* – which is another way of saying that one trusts in the law or one's good works – then Christ becomes useless. There is no compromise here. One trusts either in Christ or in circumcision.

If you trust in your ability to keep the law, then Christ cannot profit you with respect to salvation. By focusing on the law, you lose Christ. Think of it in this way. If you believe that you are good enough to get into heaven, you will feel no need of Christ. You will not look to another to grant you life eternal. This is evident from everyday life. If someone comes to me and says, 'Let me help you translate the book of Galatians,' how do I respond? I reply, 'I don't need help to do that, thanks very much. I already know how to translate the book.' If someone says to an airline pilot, 'Let me teach you to fly your plane,' his response is, 'I don't need your help to fly a plane. I am an expert.' If we think we are spiritually capable of keeping the law, we don't trust in Christ for our salvation. We depend upon ourselves and our own goodness.

But that raises a question that verse 3 answers: 'Why won't it work to trust in our obedience and our keeping of the law? Why is it foolish to trust in our good works to save us?' What if we say, 'The fact is that I am a good person! I am not stealing, murdering, or committing adultery. I am honest and honour my parents. There are wicked people in the world, but I am not one of them.' What Paul says here is quite remarkable. Those who trust in circumcision, or baptism, or any good thing they do to save them are obligated to keep the entire law.

What does Paul mean by saying that they are obligated to keep the whole law? I think his point is as follows. Those who trust in their own goodness for salvation are completely deceived. They are heading down a path that is an impossible burden.

Why is the pathway they are choosing such a burden? Because God requires that we keep the whole law in order to be saved. In other words, God doesn't grade on the curve. He requires perfection. God doesn't allow us into heaven if we keep the law most of the time: 75% of the time, or 90% of the time. No; he requires a 100% compliance. So relying on the law is a terrible burden, because we can never do what is required. It is a no-exit strategy. We enter a maze that we can never get out of.

You might say, 'This is unfair. Why does God require 100%? No one can fulfil that requirement.' That's exactly the point. God wants us to turn away from trusting in ourselves. He wants us to look entirely to Christ for our righteousness. And if we don't understand why God requires 100%, it is because we don't grasp God's perfect goodness and holiness. We are so used to looking at the smudged mirrors of our lives that we think we are good. But God's holiness is brilliant and dazzling, like sunlight hitting a mirror. We can't even look at the mirror, because its brightness is more than we can handle.

So too, God's goodness is matchless and infinite, and demands nothing less than perfection. And that perfection is ours through Jesus Christ. He lived a perfect life, so that we put our trust in him alone for our salvation. That is why Paul is so strong in his

warning in verse 4. There is no middle way: we trust for salvation
either in Christ or in the law. If we are trying to be justified (right
with God) by the law, we are cut off from Christ. If we trust in
the law for our salvation, we are no longer relying on God's grace.
Justification is no longer a gift but based also on our own efforts
and our obedience. If we trust in the law, we take away from the
glory of Christ in our salvation, for if our justification is due to our
work, then we get the glory and honour and praise. Then people
say, 'Tom Schreiner is a good man. He should go to heaven.' But
the gospel says, 'Jesus Christ is a great Saviour. He saves the worst
of sinners.'

Let's step back again and think of verses 2–4. These verses were
not written to unbelievers. They were written to the believers in
Galatia. Paul doesn't say that the Galatians *are* trusting in their
works. He *warns* them *not* to trust in their works. These verses are
not a *declaration* but a *warning*. And since Paul warns the Christians
in Galatia not to fall back into works, we need this warning too!
We also need to be admonished, so that we don't fall back, even
subtly, into trusting in ourselves. Warnings are like road signs
along the way in our Christian lives that admonish us to keep
driving in the Christian life in the right way. Paul warns us that if
we abandon Christ and turn to the law for our salvation, then we
will be damned; we will be cut off from Christ.

What if you were to object, 'But I don't need a warning like
this, because I am a true Christian and I will never fall away from
Christ. He has promised to keep me by his grace.' I agree. He has
promised to keep you by his grace. But the warnings are one of
the means God uses to keep us in the good way of trusting in
Christ. Warnings are not opposed to promises, but are one of the
means God uses to fulfil his promises. Just as road signs keep
us driving safely on the highway, so warnings remind us to keep
putting our trust in Christ.

In the last few months, we had some friends staying with us
and they parked a rented van in the back of our driveway. I joked
that one day, when pulling out of our garage, I would hit it. One

day, our family had to go somewhere in a hurry. We jumped into
our van, and I backed quickly. Suddenly John yelled out, 'Dad,
stop!' I slammed on the brakes and missed the van that was
parked out back. I had completely forgotten about it being there!
John's warning was the means by which I avoided an accident.
That's how God's warnings work, too. They prevent us from
falling away from Christ.

But how does a warning like this fit with the gospel? For it says
that if we fall away from Christ, we will be damned. Doesn't this
fill us with fear, and impel us to trust in ourselves and to rely on
our own works? God forbid! Do you not see here that the Lord
warns us against trusting in our righteousness and in our works?
We have already seen that the sin that he warns the Galatians
against is returning to the law; about trusting in themselves rather
than Christ. Paul isn't teaching works-righteousness but just the
opposite. He encourages the Galatians to turn away from the law
and to keep clinging to Christ; to keep trusting in Christ.

The warning, then, should not turn us to a kind of obsessive
perfectionism but to just the opposite. Paul admonishes us to
trust in the cross alone for our salvation; to find our righteousness in Christ alone; to turn away from ourselves to God. The
warning can be expressed this way: 'Don't trust in yourself, but
trust in Christ. Look to him alone. He is your hope, your strength
and your shield. Don't trust in your strength, your intellect, your
wisdom or your accomplishments. Look only to Christ.'

The second truth we see in this passage is that we trust in
Christ alone for our righteousness. We find this in Galatians
5:5–6. 'For through the Spirit, by faith, we ourselves eagerly wait
for the hope of righteousness. For in Christ Jesus neither circumcision nor uncircumcision counts for anything, but only faith
working through love.'

Paul often teaches that we are righteous by faith now, if we
trust in Christ. But here he is looking at the judgment day: the
day when all the secrets of men will be revealed. As believers,
we await that day eagerly and with confidence. We await that day

with confident hope. As Paul says, we have the 'hope of righteousness' on that day. Hope doesn't mean that we are uncertain about
our righteousness on the last day. It isn't like saying in August in
Louisville, Kentucky (where I live), 'I hope it won't be too hot
today.' For we all know in Louisville that it will be blazing hot in
August. But biblical hope isn't like that. Rather, we have a sure
and certain confidence and assurance that we will be declared
righteous on the last day.

Yes, we are already righteous now. The verdict of the judgment
day has been announced in advance. But we await the day when
God's verdict will be declared to the whole world, and when his
work will be completed in us. Right now we are righteous but still
sinners, but we await the day when God's work will be completed.
By faith in God's promises, we trust that God will announce to
the world what is now hidden, and that he will finish the work he
started in us.

Luther remarked:

This is a very important and pleasant comfort with which to bring
wonderful encouragement to minds afflicted and disturbed with a
sense of sin and afraid of every flaming dart of the devil . . . your
righteousness is not visible, and it is not conscious; but it is hoped for as
something to be revealed in due time. Therefore you must not judge on
the basis of your consciousness of sin, which terrifies and troubles you,
but on the basis of the promise and teaching of faith, by which Christ is
promised to you as your perfect and eternal righteousness. (21).

But what role does the Spirit have in all this? Why does Paul
say that it is 'through the Spirit . . . we await the hope of righteousness'? I think the idea is that we cannot sustain faith on our
own. Our faith is a miraculous and supernatural work of the Holy
Spirit. What an encouragement this is to me. My faith is not ultimately something I do. Our faith is the result of the Spirit's work
in us. He is the one who grants us faith. We are righteous by faith
alone and not by works. And our faith is not a work; it is the result

of the Spirit's work in us. Where does faith come from? It comes from the supernatural work of God himself.

Verse 6 confirms that righteousness is by faith alone. We aren't righteous based on our obedience to the law. Being circumcised, going to church, reading the Bible, and being a good person do not avail before God. But neither is God impressed if we don't do religious rituals. We can also become proud of the fact that we are not focused on externals. We may become proud of the fact that we are theologically astute enough to know that circumcision is not required, and that we don't keep the food laws. Works-righteousness is incredibly subtle, because we may begin to think we are especially godly because we understand the doctrines of grace, and we know that righteousness is by faith alone, and we reject views that are wrong.

The only thing that matters before God, however, is faith. Faith means that we trust God in Christ for everything. Faith means that we are always holding up to God an empty hand. I want to be strong and capable and a can-do kind of person. But faith alone is important, because it reminds us that we are weak and needy and that we need him every hour. Do you ever get tired of the trials in your life, and look forward to the day when everything is going great? Thank God for the trials, because they remind you that you need him every hour, and that righteousness is by faith alone.

Luther said:

> in the conflicts and fears that continually return to plague you, you should patiently look with hope for the righteousness that you have only by faith, though only in an incipient and imperfect form, until it is revealed perfectly and eternally in due time. 'But I am not conscious of having righteousness, or at least I am only dimly conscious of it!' You are not to be conscious of having righteousness; you are to believe it. And unless you believe that you are righteous, you insult and blaspheme Christ, who has cleansed you by the washing of water with the Word (Eph 5:26) and who in His death on the cross condemned and killed sin and death, so that through Him you might obtain eternal

righteousness and life. You cannot deny this, unless you want to be
obviously wicked, blasphemous, and contemptuous of God, of all the
divine promises, of Christ, and of all His benefits. (26–27).

And Paul in this verse tells us something else that is very important. Faith expresses itself in love. We are not justified by our love
but by our faith. Faith is the root and love is the fruit. Our love
flows from our faith. So we should never say that our justification
is based on our love, or on any other good thing we do. But faith
is a living and active thing. It produces good fruit. When we trust
God for our lives, then we are freed from the worry of thinking
about ourselves all the time. We are set free to love others and to
care for them.

# INDEX OF SCRIPTURE REFERENCES

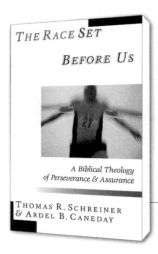

# THE RACE SET BEFORE US

*A Biblical Theology
of Perseverance & Assurance*

THOMAS R. SCHREINER
& ARDEL B. CANEDAY

The Christian life is like a racecourse, a marathon, set out before us. There is a reward in running well but particularly in finishing. Christians agree that this is a consistent pattern of New Testament teaching.

But is the prize an extra bonus, a reward for having finished well? Or is the prize salvation itself? And if the prize is salvation, can it be lost? Or is everyone who has signed up and started the race guaranteed a share in the prize –

even if they quit before the end or follow a different course?

In this exploration of biblical theology of perseverance and assurance, Thomas Schreiner and Ardel Caneday weigh and consider all of the relevant New Testament texts. Applying sound principles of biblical interpretation and conversing with recent evangelical thought, they give us a foundational study with profound spiritual implications for Christian living and pastoral ministry.

ISBN:
978-0-85111-551-1

Available from your local Christian bookshop
or via our website at **www.ivpbooks.com**

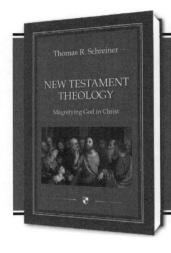

## A Higher Throne
*Evangelicals and Public Theology*
Chris Green (editor)
ISBN: 978-1-84474-277-6

A lively conversation among those who represent a consistently orthodox evangelicalism, who see public life in relation to the Christian gospel in quite different ways, but who are committed to thinking biblically about it and coming to a common mind.

## Engaging with the Holy Spirit
*Six crucial questions*
Graham A. Cole
ISBN: 978-1-84474-179-3

Graham Cole's study focuses on important questions of practical relevance. Each one confronts us with challenges about our relationship with the Spirit, whether as Christian believers or unbelievers.

## God's Power to Save
*One gospel for a complex world?*
Chris Green (editor)
ISBN: 978-1-84474-134-2

In the New Testament, do the Synoptic Gospels and John, or the Synoptic Gospels and Paul, or indeed Paul and Jesus, have such mutually exclusive views that they are not coherent in diversity, but actually divergent? These questions are subjected to penetrating, rigorous analysis.

www.ivpbooks.com

For more details of books published by IVP, visit our website where you will find all the latest information, including:

Book extracts            Downloads
Author interviews        Online bookshop
Reviews                  Christian bookshop finder

You can also sign up for our regular email newsletters, which are tailored to your particular interests, and tell others what you think about this book by posting a review.

We publish a wide range of books on various subjects including:

Christian living          Small-group resources
Key reference works       Topical issues
Bible commentary series   Theological studies